Change for Children

IDEAS AND ACTIVITIES FOR INDIVIDUALIZING LEARNING

CHANGE FOR CHILDREN

Ideas and Activities for Individualizing Learning

Sandra Nina Kaplan
Jo Ann Butom Kaplan
Sheila Kunishima Madsen
Bette Taylor Gould

Scott, Foresman and Company
Glenview, IL London

78910-BKC-9089888786
ISBN: 0-673-16348-2

Contents

Preface

We recognize that the importance of individualizing instruction has not changed through the years. However, we also recognize that the interests and needs of children and teachers do change over time. It has also been brought to our attention that the information and activities within the first edition of *Change for Children* were equally applicable to teachers in traditional as well as open classrooms. These factors and the suggestions from readers led to our decision to revise this book. This edition of *Change for Children* retains information and activities most helpful to implement individualization of instruction and adds new information and activities for the children and teachers of today.

The changes included within this second edition of *Change for Children* are:

new learning centers

new activities in learning centers from the first edition

revisions of steps to develop and use a learning center

addition of new skills and procedures for independent study

all new, full-size reproducible worksheets

restructured chapters for easier use.

The activities and techniques presented in this book provide a guide and model for teachers to individualize learning within their classrooms. They provide a step-by-step approach to changing the classroom environment, developing and placing learning activities in the room, and devising plans and schedules of student and teacher time. In addition, guides are presented for developing an independent study program. Ideas for record keeping and evaluation complete the total program of individualizing learning.

These activities are not intended to put teachers into a mold, but rather to help them create their own individualized learning program. Teachers may choose those parts of the book which are most appropriate for their student and teacher needs and interests.

Many of the techniques for individualizing learning have been presented in a step-by-step format. However, not all the steps may be used by all children. The individual differences of children will determine which steps they will use and the order in which they will use them.

The success we had in initiating an individualized learning program was based on the ideas and techniques presented in this book. After working with teachers and hearing their pleas for concrete methods to help them begin programs of their own, we decided to make our ideas available. We hope that the following pages will be an aid to teachers who want to make the transition from knowing about individualized learning to practicing individualized learning.

Introduction

DEFINING INDIVIDUALIZED LEARNING

Personalized Instruction

Stylized Learning

Humanized Education

Open Structure

Individualized Instruction

Custom-tailored Learning

Educators have coined many terms to describe what they mean by individualized learning. As it applies to the ideas and techniques presented in this book, individualized learning is the process of developing and retaining *individuality* by a classroom organization that provides for the effective and efficient learning experiences of *each* class member. Teaching and learning methods which focus on the total class are replaced by those which cater to individual differences. The need to label and categorize students in order to attend to their differences is lessened when each class member is attended to as an individual. Individualized learning comes about by varying the teaching and learning processes according to the interests, preferences, sociometrics, learning styles, and abilities and achievements of the students.

Adding the word individualized to learning does not mean that the teacher instructs every child individually, nor does it mean that group instruction is taboo. Grouping students for academic and social learning is a necessary component of an individualized classroom. Learning to interact, cooperate, and work as a group member is vital to the development of each child as an individual. Flexible groups which pull students together for a specific purpose aid the teacher in individualizing learning. Students should be members of various groups in order to have various experiences. The goal is to insure that no child becomes a permanent member of either a high, average, or low group.

THE CHANGE PROCESS

The provision of a wide range of materials and activities to create an indoor/outdoor learning environment.

The appropriateness of activities for different types of students.

The opportunities for students to make decisions about what they learn.

The teacher's interaction with students based on knowledge of the learning process.

These are the benchmarks for assessing whether the teacher has made the transition to an individualized learning classroom.

Rearranging the furniture

Stuffing the room with things

Allowing students to move about the room

These changes do not insure that a teacher is individualizing learning. What is visible in the classroom cannot be used as the measure for determining the effectiveness of the teaching/learning process. The teacher must focus attention on how students learn rather than on the content of the subjects taught. The teacher must become a specialist in relationships: child to child, child to teacher, and child to learning. By interacting with students while promoting learning the teacher becomes the intermediary between the child and his environment. He must question, encourage, conference, and share. In this way, he will help make the environment useful for the student. Although the teacher's age, experience, and training are the basis for his authority in the classroom, he must exercise this authority to make learning available to students rather than to impose it on them.

EXPECTATIONS AND EVALUATION

The number of changes which take place is not important. How fast things change in the process of individualizing learning is not important. What is important is that the teacher can answer these questions for himself:

Why am I doing this?

What do I hope to accomplish by this action?

How do I feel about what will be changed?

Success is determined by the teacher's ability to decide what needs to be changed and how these changes can be implemented. Introspection will determine the teacher's tolerance for student noise, mobility, and decision making in the assessment of how much change is acceptable. The teacher needs to develop a philosophical framework from which he can operate. An understanding of why changes are made substantiates these changes to the students, their parents, and the teacher's colleagues.

"My class was choosing the same activities, turning in sloppy work, and using materials in the same way day after day. I had so much fear of manipulating children and of imposing my standards on them that I did nothing at all. I thought that when the time was right for them they would come to me, or they would discover what they needed for themselves. I just decided that I had a responsibility to step in and provide what they were asking for and what I felt was necessary for them at the time."

Individualizing learning does not imply that the teacher will abdicate the responsibility for making some decisions and directing some learnings for the students. The teacher must decide when and where to function as a group member or group leader. Nor does it mean that the teacher will allow or accept anything students do. The goal of individualized learning is to create new standards for learning and behavior, not to abolish or disregard all standards. As the adult, facilitator, friend, and teacher, he is still accountable for the behavior and performance of his students. Teacher accountability assumes a different dimension in the individualized classroom. Although not accountable for teaching all the students the same body of knowledge and skills, he is accountable for teaching each student how to direct his learning in relationship to his individual learning style and needs. In an individualized learning classroom, the major emphasis in evaluating students is on the processes of learning, not on the products of learning. This does not exclude the fact that in any type of learning environment, the students must learn basic and fundamental skills.

"After two years of trial and error in moving into individualizing, I really thought I was ready for my third year. So I set up the environment, gave children the opportunity to make choices, made a variety of materials and working spaces available, and readied myself for that first day. After a month we were still in an unhappy state of chaos. I had ignored the most important factor: the children—a set of students who had had little experience with making choices and assuming real responsibility at school. They seemed to need support and training in how to make appropriate decisions and carry through on commitments. I realized that they needed to go through the same process that I had gone through: taking small steps and beginning with one area. We set up a decision-making center where all the activities were geared to teach and reinforce the process of decision

making. We had lots of class meetings, some with imaginary situations and others with actual happenings in our class. We began some self-scheduling for one time block a day. Slowly, I gave and they accepted and asked for more responsibility."

Students cannot be expected to change just because the classroom environment and the teacher have changed. Not all students will be ready or able to adjust themselves to some or all aspects of an individualized learning classroom. The teacher must exercise judgment in order to determine which students manifest the maturity and skill to function successfully in this type of learning environment. The skills needed to work in an individualized classroom must be taught and practiced in the same way other subject area skills are taught and practiced.

"'This has been one hell of a week. . . . You name it, it's happened. I'm going back to straight rows and three-group reading.'

This kind of feeling has come up more than once in this process of change I've been going through. At these times I've found it necessary to pull in the reins and set up tighter limits and standards. Somehow, just naturally, I find myself and the class moving out again into a more open situation. These periods of pulling in, at least for me, seem to provide a time for some stability and reevaluation of what might have been going wrong. In other words a few setbacks don't mean you're a failure. They may help you eventually move further ahead."

The students and teacher try and evaluate, move ahead and step back. This is the process of making the transition to an individualized classroom. Opportunities for the class to share and discuss their frustrations, concerns, failures, and successes are important in making the change process understood and effective.

THE LEARNING CENTER APPROACH TO INDIVIDUALIZING LEARNING

The development and use of learning centers is only one method for individualizing learning. They provide a beginning point but are not intended to be the only source of individualizing instruction. Learning centers become the vehicles for moving students away from teacher-dominated learning experiences and toward student-selected learning activities. Learning centers organize and direct learning experiences for students by allowing freedom while providing structure.

FLOW CHART

The flow chart that follows identifies the elements of learning centers and presents a pattern for selecting and using these centers. This flow chart illustrates the relationship of these elements in a particular pattern. However, there are a variety of ways to sequence these elements to use learning centers effectively. The elements represent divisions of the book in which the teacher can find a collection of examples. Thus, the flow chart can be helpful to teachers as an outline to follow when using the book, as well as a guide to follow when using learning centers.

FLOW CHART

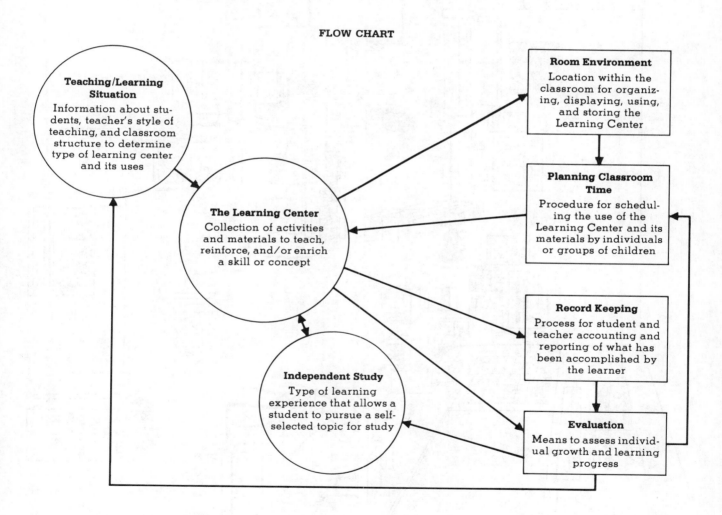

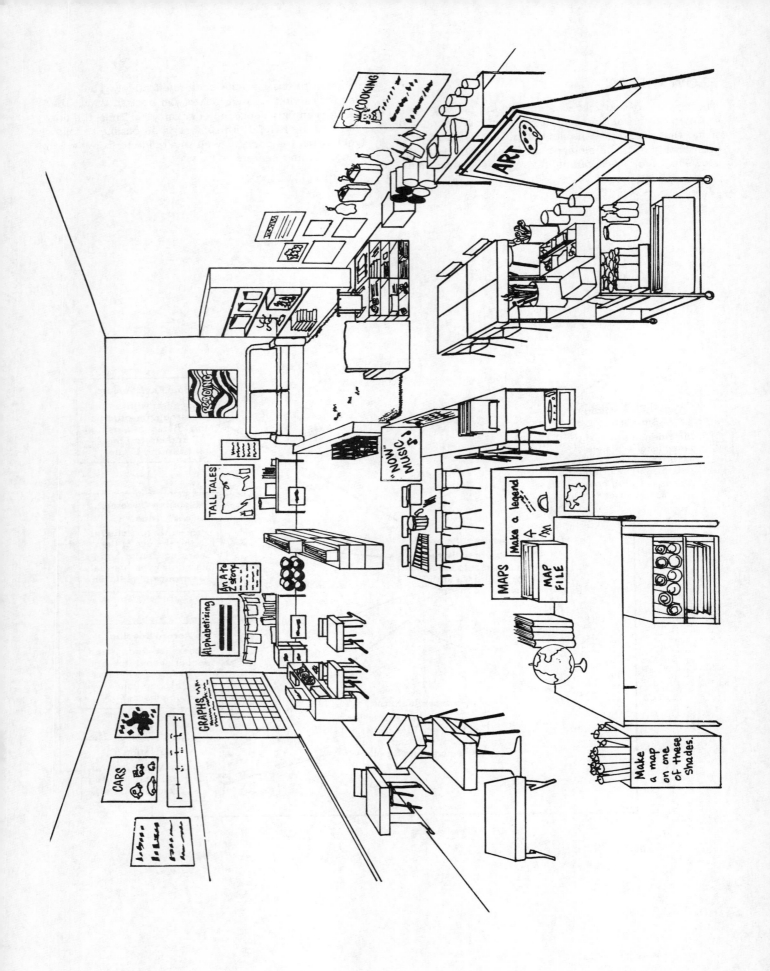

1
Room Environment and Room Organization

THE ENVIRONMENT AS A LEARNING CATALYST

The environment of a classroom does not just happen. It is a carefully planned and organized structure that provides stimulation and challenge and also meets the needs and interests of the students. What is placed in the room and how it is arranged determine the atmosphere for learning and allow students freedom to move, both academically and physically. The room becomes a source for initiating and organizing learning activities; therefore, what is included and its availability to the students are of primary importance. Every part of the room should be considered as having potential for student experience or learning. The room environment becomes a resource for promoting social, emotional, and academic growth.

The confines of the classroom represent only one type of environment in which children can learn. The environment outside the classroom must also be considered as a resource for learning. For students in an individualized program of instruction, the optimum learning environment is one which integrates the classroom with the school, the home, and the community.

The following checklist may be used as a guide in planning a new or changing room environment or for periodic assessments of an existing one.

ROOM ENVIRONMENT CHECKLIST

Areas for independent work

Small-group instruction areas

Places for student-to-student interaction

Area convenient for meeting with the entire class

Balance between quiet and noisy work areas

Signs and labels for different areas

Directions posted for using each area

Materials labeled, organized, and available to children

Variety of raw materials

Balance between the use of commercial materials, teacher- or student-made materials, and objects from the real world

Places for children to display their work

Displays of children's work

Maintenance and cleanup system

Frequent change of displays and centers

Free flow of traffic

Areas outside of the classroom used as a part of the total environment

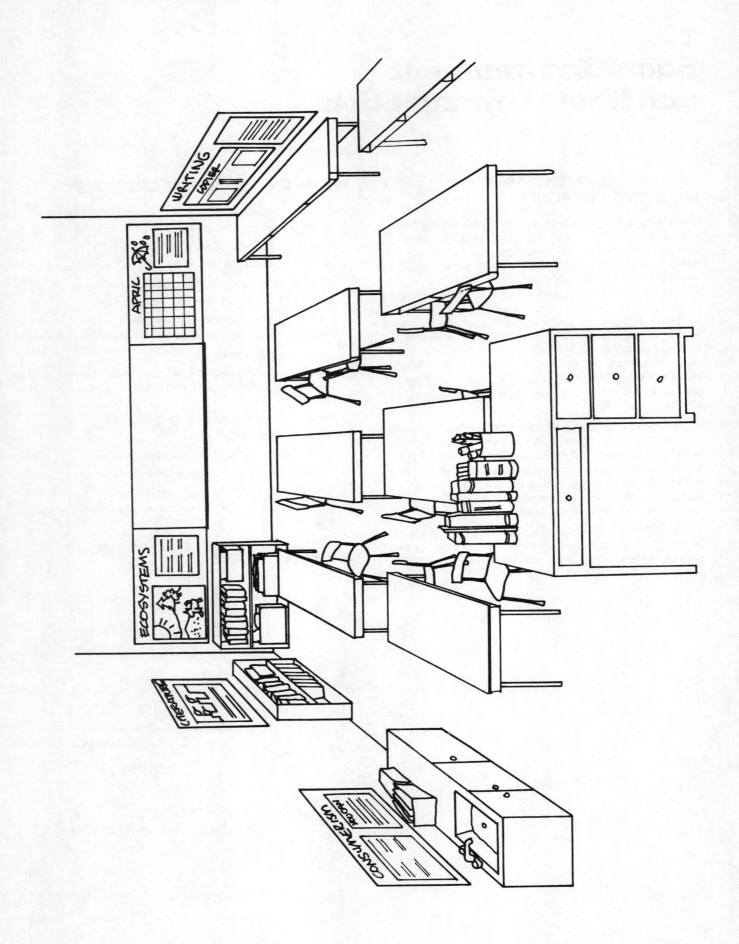

CREATING CLASSROOM SECTIONS

Sectioning parts of the room into learning centers and working areas helps to make more efficient use of classroom space while providing an atmosphere where children can be actively involved in learning. Such areas can be created without the use of special equipment or materials by rearranging existing classroom furniture. A bookcase, file cabinet, chart rack, or piano can partition off an area; desks and chairs can be grouped to form an area; and colored cloth tape can be used to define an area. Establishing nooks and crannies within the classroom creates an environment which serves the needs of children: a place to talk, a space to be alone, a place to work with friends, a place to work quietly, a place to be lively, and a place to sit and think.

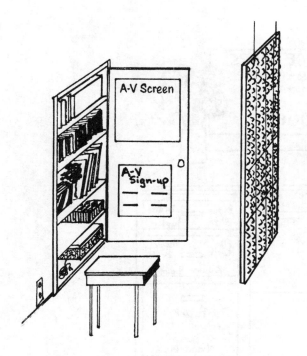

Cloth Divider

An artistic and utilitarian room divider is formed by hanging cloth from the ceiling of the classroom. Pieces of doweling are glued or sewn to each end of the material and suspended from the ceiling or lights by string or wire. The cloth divider also functions as a display area.

Box Office

Cut out the top, bottom, and one side of a large cardboard box to form a portable office where students can work alone. Students can also build and decorate their own box offices.

Teacher's Desk

The teacher's desk can be used by students as an extra place to store and file materials. The top of the desk becomes a student office.

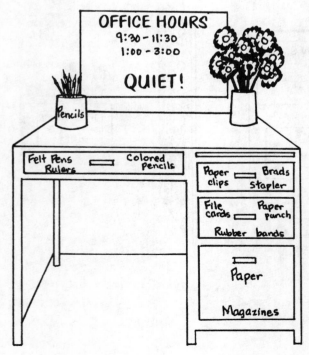

Closet Door

An open closet door can be used as a bulletin board or as a screen for viewing filmstrips. The closet space is used as an additional work or storage area, or a place for a learning center. Placing tables and chairs adjacent to the closet further enhances its usability.

Egg Carton

A room divider is built by joining egg cartons with brads, pipe cleaners, or staples. Each child can decorate an egg carton for the divider. The completed divider is suspended from the ceiling or supported by blocks of wood at the base.

Chipboard Divider

A divider made of durable cardboard is used as a bulletin board. Placing it between two tables makes two work or display areas.

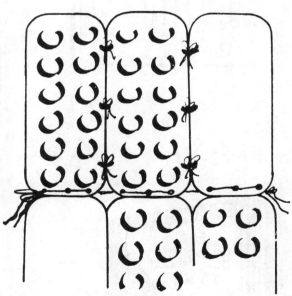

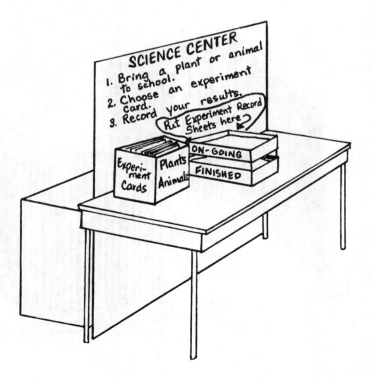

"Casablanca" Room Divider

A room divider is made by stringing together bottle caps, jar lids, pop tops, and paper clips. This divider can be educational as well as functional when used with counting, estimating, and big-numbers activities.

Room Divider

A nurse's screen or a flannel board is a ready-made divider that can be used to section off areas in the classroom. Making areas or corners out of open spaces provides for individual and group activities. The dividers themselves can function as display areas for student and teacher work.

Corrugated Booth

Corrugated paper can be used to design areas for students to work independently, to find quiet, or to isolate themselves from the group. The paper is taped along a table top to form individual study booths.

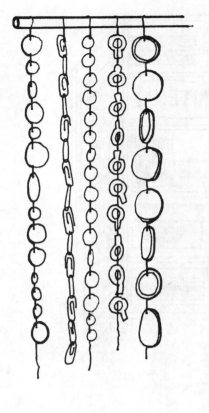

THE READING CORNER

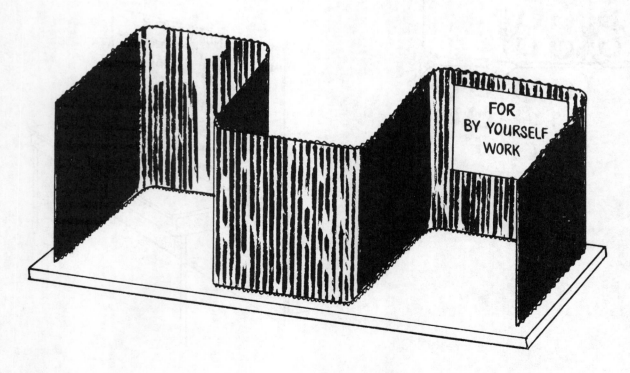

FOR BY YOURSELF WORK

SIGNS AND LABELS

Posting signs and labeling areas focus the students' attention on what and where things are in the room. Because signs and labels function like maps to direct students on their learning course, the teacher is free to spend more time on instruction. Use of signs also reinforces the skill of following and interpreting directions from written messages. Labeling and designating various areas of the classroom further the goal of developing self-directed learners.

Bulletin Board Box

A storage area and bulletin board are made by standing the lid of a dress or shirt box against the bottom of the box. Messages written or pinned on the bulletin board (lid) relate to the materials that are placed in the box.

Labeling a Center

The area on which a learning center will be displayed is covered with paper. A diagram is drawn on the paper to indicate where each of the materials for the center will be placed. Students can thus easily assume responsibility for the care of materials and the orderliness of the center.

Footprint Sign

Footprints cut and taped to the floor capture interest and direct students to an area in the classroom. Let students use their own feet as patterns.

Sign Post

Made of paper, doweling, and clay, sign posts call attention to working spaces or materials.

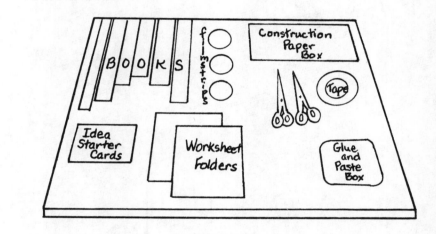

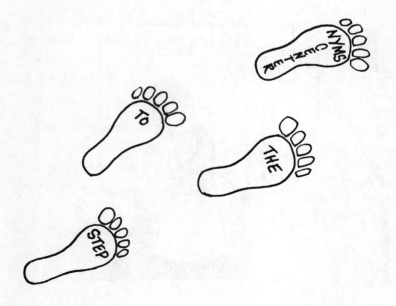

Poster

Posters made from heavy paper and posted or hung at the activities area help students to identify and locate the alternatives which are available to them. Artistically done posters magnetize students toward them and provide additional decor for the classroom.

3-D Signs

Three-dimensional signs are made by gluing objects to cardboard. The materials used to create the signs can relate to the learning center topic or subject matter displayed—aluminum cans for conservation; leaves, twigs, dried flowers for nature; and wrappers and containers for consumerism.

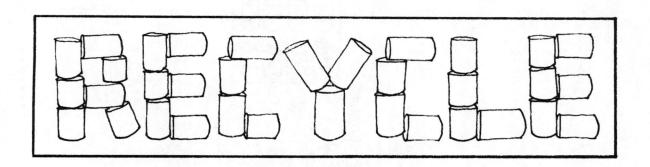

WAYS TO STORE MATERIALS

In order to allow students to become independent workers while maintaining an orderly classroom, the teacher needs to provide various ways to store materials. When materials are stored openly, children are able to direct their own activity without relying on the teacher. Careful labeling and placing of storage holders develops the students' awareness of where things can be found and how things should be kept, and reinforces student responsibility.

Bottle Box

A divided carton with each section identified by labels makes a handy storage cupboard. Supplies, student projects, or materials can be placed in the bottle box.

Sawhorse

A sawhorse turned upside down makes an ideal place to file cumbersome pictures and projects on a permanent or temporary basis. Its legs form bookends which can hold large pieces of chipboard, cardboard, and paper. Pieces of cardboard labeled with children's names can be used as dividers for this filing cabinet.

File Box

File boxes made out of cardboard boxes covered with wrapping or contact paper contain the materials for a specific curriculum area. Folders in the file box are labeled and placed in a meaningful sequence. A corrected example of each worksheet should be placed in the folder so that students can assume the responsibility for self-checking.

Storage/Display Box

A box with the top removed becomes a storage container as well as a multisided display unit. Learning center materials can be stored inside the box. Signs, directions, task cards, and worksheets can be stapled, glued, or placed in envelopes on the sides.

Cubbies

Produce boxes can be used as children's lockers, as bookcases, or as storage bins. Knock out one side; then sand and paint them. They can be stacked and held secure with heavy-duty staples, nails driven in at an angle, or a strip of wood attached along the side.

Shoe Holder

Dimestore shoe holders are used as storage centers for supplies or learning activity cards. Labeling the pockets helps the class locate and return materials.

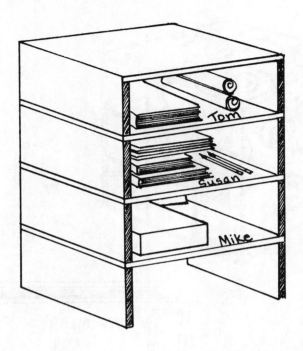

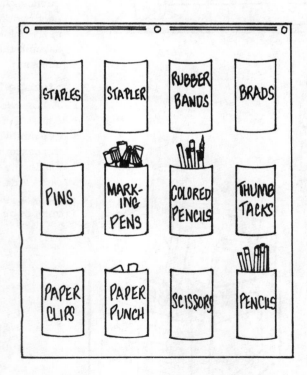

DISPLAYING WORK FOR CHILDREN

Making materials accessible to students is an essential part of helping them become self-directed. It also reinforces the development of student decision-making skills and encourages responsibility. Careful and artistic placement of materials serves to motivate students to use the materials and provides a model for students to follow when they are responsible for setting up displays of their own.

DISPLAYING WORK OF CHILDREN

The classroom environment should reflect the students who live and work in it. Displaying children's work gives recognition to each child, provides a stimulus for others to study the same topic or make similar products, and serves as an informational resource. Exhibits should be changed frequently and include the work of all children.

Wall Hanging

A piece of fabric stretched between two pieces of doweling serves as an additional bulletin board on which items may be displayed.

Clothesline

Tape or tack up colored yarn to make a clothesline to display activities for children or work completed by children. Paper or plastic bags can be used to hold art supplies, worksheets, or task cards for children to use.

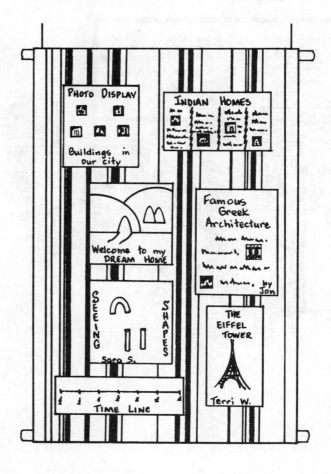

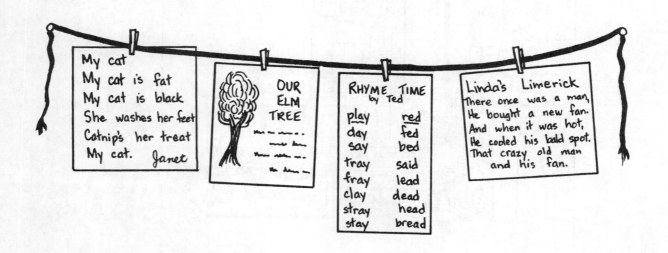

Refrigerator Box

A large box provides a free-standing display area. It can be moved to different locations within the room to become part of any learning or work center.

Cardboard Backdrop

Sheets of cardboard or plywood are hinged together with masking tape to form a portable display unit. It can also be used as a screen to section off areas on a table or on the floor.

Cutting Board

A pattern cutting board covered with adhesive paper, wallpaper, or colored construction paper provides several panels as well as a front and a back for displaying children's work or other materials.

Chalkboard

Section off an unused portion of the chalkboard and cover it with a large sheet of butcher paper by pinning or stapling it to the frame of the chalkboard. Children's work is taped or glued to the paper. The butcher paper can be easily removed from the chalkboard and the display transferred to a hallway, another classroom, the library, or office.

Styrofoam Panels

Large panels of styrofoam covered with fabric or spray-painted make lightweight display units and can be easily attached to most surfaces.

They are ideal for setting up displays of children's work in areas other than the classroom.

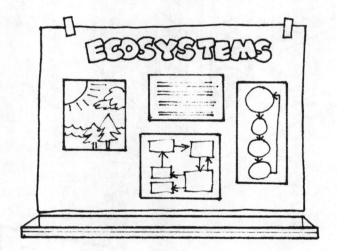

GETTING THINGS THAT ARE NEEDED FOR THE CLASSROOM

The concept of the *everywhere classroom* is that teachers and students can find tools and materials for learning everywhere—in the community, neighborhood, and home. Finding these resources develops the students' awareness of their environment and introduces them to new people, new experiences, and new materials. It is also a way to involve parents and the community in a school's program.

Resource File

A resource file can be established to extend learnings beyond the limits of the classroom, the teacher's area of knowledge, and the reading material available at given levels. The need and use of such a file arises from student interest, independent study topics, and learning center themes and activities. The responsibility for soliciting resources should be both the teacher's and the student's. As resources are identified, the pertinent information is recorded on cards. This file enables students to have firsthand experiences by visiting places and to have direct contact with people who offer expertise.

GARDENS - vegetables	
Human Resources	**Materials Available**
Demonstration of planting, caring for plants, harvesting Mrs. G. available on Tu, Thurs. 10-11 a.m.	Samples of seeds, plant leaves, stems, flowers
Visit to Mrs. G's garden- limit: 6 students per time call to set up time	Types of gardening tools- some available for short term loan
Call for information anytime	Samples of fertilizers and soils for experiments.
Mrs. Gary - 624 Blue St. - phone: 624-3185	

CONSTRUCTION	Building Materials
Human Resources	**Materials Available**
Bring & talk about building materials - Mr. Jones available Mon. afternoons	wood scraps, old nails, screws talk to Mr. Lee, ext. 45
Teaching sawing, nailing, drilling, etc. Mr. Lee call to arrange time	old linoleum samples, formica samples, broken bricks talk to Mr. Jones
Tour through Company - Mr. Zee call for appointment	
XYZ BUILDING SUPPLIES	262 hwh Blvd - phone 326-2387

Store-Bought Materials

A myriad of storage containers in different shapes and sizes can be purchased in stores, rummage or garage sales, and thrift shops.

plastic stackables
plastic jars
laundry baskets
divided trays
see-through shoe boxes
wastebaskets
utility drawers
plastic carry-alls with
    several compartments
utility boxes
Zip-loc bags
plastic food-storage con-
    tainers
buckets

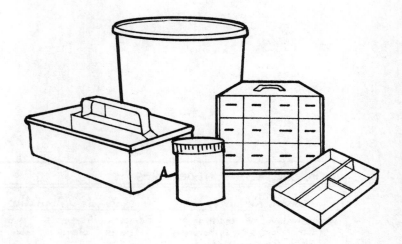

The smaller containers are ideal for storing multiples of the same item such as beads, buttons, pipecleaners, macaroni, fabric scraps, etc., or for items that come with several pieces—puzzles and games. Larger containers can be used for unwieldy items—wood scraps, individual or group projects.

Store-"Borrowed" Materials

Stores, merchants, and manufacturers are sources for display items and raw materials. Merchants periodically discard display racks, shelves, and promotional displays, which can be used in the classroom to store or show off materials. Check with local manufacturers and shops for scrap materials. They can provide you and your students with a variety of "new" raw materials with which to work.

CALLING ALL Parents, Grandparents, neighbors, interested adults...

Dear Parents,

Can you HELP us??? You may be surprised at the ways you can help and how much fun you'll have doing it. We already have 3 parents who are donating their time and resources. Don't worry about how much time you can give or how regularly you can come. We'll work something out.

Following is a list of some of the ways you can help us. Maybe you have other ideas as well. Please check the areas where you can help and return this form to school with your child tomorrow.

Thank you for your cooperation and interest.

Mrs. Jones

These materials will be used by the children and will not be returned, so don't give us your best!

_____ tin cans and plastic containers with lids
_____ cooking utensils (mixing bowls, measuring cups and spoons, etc.)
_____ lumber odds and ends, nails, screws
_____ tools (hammer, saw, pliers, screwdrivers)
_____ anything styrofoam (egg cartons, packing materials, etc.)
_____ needles and thread, spools, buttons
_____ T.V. dinner trays   _____ meat trays
_____ yarn and yardage scraps   _____ embroidery hoops
_____ rugs   _____ used furniture
_____ broken appliances

I can donate my time in the following ways:

_____ help with clerical work (type stories at home, copy dittoes, etc.)
_____ help in the classroom with small groups (no special skills needed)
_____ help at the cooking center
_____ help at the stitch and sew center
_____ help children learn to shoot baskets, bat balls, jump rope, etc.)
_____ help supervise on field trips and neighborhood walks
_____ share a hobby, skill, interest or profession with the children
_____ listen to an individual child read
_____ take cans and bottles to the reclamation center

_____
Parent's signature

Scavenger Hunts

Scavenger hunts can be used as means of obtaining materials needed in the classroom or in combination with a particular skill under study. For example, to reinforce measurement, all objects to be collected are listed with specific measurements—2 meters of red yarn; to teach reading comprehension, objects are described rather than named—a container for ovoid objects that originate in a chicken.

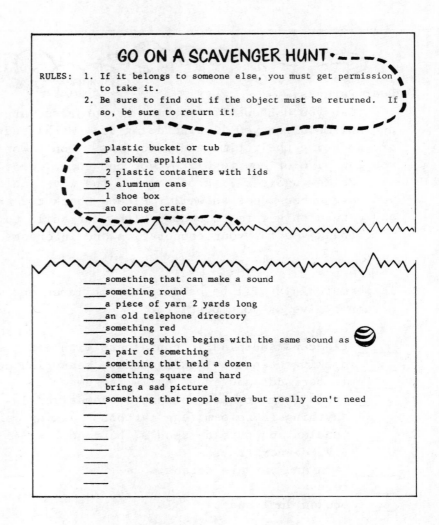

GO ON A SCAVENGER HUNT

RULES: 1. If it belongs to someone else, you must get permission to take it.
2. Be sure to find out if the object must be returned. If so, be sure to return it!

____plastic bucket or tub
____a broken appliance
____2 plastic containers with lids
____5 aluminum cans
____1 shoe box
____an orange crate

____something that can make a sound
____something round
____a piece of yarn 2 yards long
____an old telephone directory
____something red
____something which begins with the same sound as
____a pair of something
____something that held a dozen
____something square and hard
____bring a sad picture
____something that people have but really don't need
____
____
____
____
____
____
____

2
How to Develop and Use Learning Centers

WHAT IS A LEARNING CENTER?

Definition of a Learning Center

A learning center is an area in the classroom which contains a collection of activities and materials to teach, reinforce, and enrich a skill or concept.

Some terms related to "Learning Center" and in some cases interchangeable with are:

learning center—a room in a school that sets up centers and independent study materials for use by children from the whole school.

learning resource room—same as above; often run by a specially trained resource specialist.

learning station—a packet, folder, or display of materials and activities usually based on a more specific skill or content, often with a smaller range and variety of materials.

interest center—often more content related; set up with realia and resources to motivate a group of children to pursue an interest independently.

discovery center or *exploration center*—usually a collection of real things and equipment set up with a starter question or task that encourages a child to play with and dabble in topics and skills; children discover their own ways of doing things and their own answers to questions.

Valuing center—activities that focus on the affective domain: emotions, feelings, attitudes.

Key Points of a Learning Center

A learning center has a variety of activities for the children to perform.

The activities and materials within a learning center range from simple to difficult and from concrete to abstract.

A learning center is geared to the abilities, interests, and needs of students within the classroom.

The materials and activities of a learning center appeal to various learning styles: kinesthetic, aural, visual, etc., and ask for a variety of responses: written, spoken, pictorial, etc.

Basic Ingredients for a Learning Center

Every learning center should contain:

multimedia materials to support the topic, theme, concept, or skill (slides, filmstrips, books, records).

manipulative materials for exploration and discovery.

Every learning center needs the reinforcement of:

a teacher's introduction to what the center contains and how it can be used.

a classroom organizational pattern which tells children when to use it.

a method for collecting, displaying, reviewing, and evaluating children's work and center materials.

Using a Learning Center

For the student the learning center is used as:

a self-selected activity to use independently.

follow-up of a teacher-taught lesson.

an activity in place of a regular assignment.

an enrichment activity.

For the teacher the learning center is used as:

follow-up to reinforce or extend a lesson.

a small-group instruction area.

an individualized activity.

a place where aides and tutors can work with students, using well-defined materials and activities.

A STEP-BY-STEP APPROACH TO CREATING A LEARNING CENTER

The following chart shows the sequence of steps involved in developing learning centers. Examples have been given for each of four different starting points. Other starting points may be used, although the general sequence of development will remain the same.

THE TEACHER'S ROLE IN A LEARNING CENTER

Preparing Introducing Encouraging Accounting

The basic assumption when defining the teacher's role in a learning center is that a learning center does not have its own lifeline: it is dependent on the teacher as a source of energy to keep it alive and functioning.

Teacher Learning Center Checklist

The teacher should prepare all the learning tools, such as worksheets and games, and collect all available resources for the center so that it contains all the necessary equipment for students to discover, learn, and apply the concept or skill for which it was developed.

A STEP-BY-STEP APPROACH TO CREATING A LEARNING CENTER

1. SELECT A STARTING POINT	**2.** DETERMINE RELATED SKILLS AND/OR CONTENT TO BE TAUGHT, REINFORCED, OR ENRICHED.	**3.** DEVELOP THE SKILL OR CONCEPT INTO A LEARNING ACTIVITY. Manipulating (cutting, pasting, matching, etc.), experimenting (observing, charting, keeping a log, etc.) listening, viewing.	**4.** TRANSLATE THE SKILL OR CONCEPT INTO AN APPLYING ACTIVITY. Filling in, arranging in order, putting together, taking apart, listing, classifying, tracing, writing, locating, labeling.
Start with a subject area. *Example:* READING	rhyming skills	Students will learn about rhyming by listening to a tape of rhymes and matching rhyming words to rhyming pictures.	Students will apply the rhyming skill to games or worksheets that ask them to fill in the rhyming words, list words that rhyme, and classify words with the same rhyming sounds.
Start with a skill area. *Example:* LINEAR MEASUREMENT, METRIC	measurement abbreviations using tools (meter stick, meter tape) figuring perimeters comparing with American Standard measures — yards, inches, feet, etc.	*Students will learn metric abbreviations by viewing filmstrip and writing each measurement when used.	*Students will apply their knowledge of abbreviations by playing the Metric Measurement Maze Game.
Start with an interest demonstrated by a portion of the class. *Example:* VOYAGER II SPACE PROBE	what Voyager II looks like what Voyager II is expected to accomplish reasons we explore space other space exploration projects.	*Using magazine and newspaper pictures as references, students will diagram and label the main parts of Voyager II.	*Students will take apart and correctly reassemble the Voyager II puzzle pieces.
Start with a theme or an issue. *Example:* People from different cultures have similar needs.	People need customs to express their commonality. People develop ways to explain the mysteries of nature. People need shelter from the elements. People need food.	*Students will learn about the customs of Mexican-Americans, Navajos and Black Americans by viewing/ listening to the Ethnic Customs filmstrip and record.	*Students will apply knowledge of ethnic customs by gluing or drawing pictures on the Customs Classification Worksheet.

*Examples have been given for the first skill or content area listed in Column 2. For a complete center, other activities are developed for each of the skill/content areas to be covered.

5. INCORPORATE THE SKILL OR CONCEPT INTO AN EXTENDING ACTIVITY.	**6.** DETERMINE WHICH ROOM AREA AND FURNITURE WILL "HOUSE" THE CENTER AND PLACE ALL THE GAMES, WORKSHEETS, CHARTS, ETC., THERE FOR CHILDREN TO USE IN A SELF-SELECTED MANNER.	**7.** COLLECT RAW MATERIALS, REAL OBJECTS, BOOKS, MEDIA ITEMS, AND RESOURCES AND PLACE AT THE CENTER.	**8.** DEVELOP RECORD-KEEPING AND EVALUATION MATERIALS AND A PROCEDURE FOR USING THEM.
Comparing, researching, reconstruction, finding what other, developing your own, or deciding what if, etc.			
Students will extend their skill of rhyming by writing their own poem, finding out about Walter de la Mare, or rewriting a nursery rhyme.	Use the top two shelves of the bookshelf in the Reading Corner for the Rhyming Center.	*Collect:* rhyming picture cards poetry books poetry tapes and filmstrips rhyming worksheets Rhyme-Time Game	Set up folders for students' use. Make booklets for students to write original poetry in. Develop a rhyming word pre/post test.
*Students will extend their use of metric abbreviations by comparing metric lengths to American Standard abbreviations by charting known lengths: such as, student's own height, foot length, etc.	Use bottom shelf of rolling cart to store measurement equipment. Store task cards, worksheets, etc. in box and place on top shelf of cart.	*Collect:* objects to measure filmstrips measuring tools Metric Measurement Maze Game Metric Study Prints	Ditto copies of My Measurement Book for each student. Make list of measurement tasks for children to do to demonstrate mastery.
*Students will extend their knowledge of the parts of Voyager II by comparing its parts with the parts of the Lunar Roving Vehicle used in the Apollo Program.	Set up Voyager II Center at Science area bulletin board. Put two-station table in front of bulletin board for materials.	*Collect:* newspapers and magazines that contain Voyager articles, pictures NASA materials on other space projects Voyager II puzzle space vehicle models	Ditto copies of Voyager II Space Log. Make up Voyager II Scientist Questionnaire to use as test.
*Students will do research to find customs of one of the ethnic groups in their background and make a chart of them.	Put materials in large box. Post tasks and staple worksheet envelopes to outside of box.	*Collect:* books Ethnic Customs Filmstrip and record realia related to customs tape and tape recorder for interviewing people of different backgrounds.	Make a class Cultural Dictionary booklet with several pages for each cultural group. Make up a picture-paragraph matching ditto to be used to check students' mastery of content.

The teacher should thoroughly introduce the learning center to the students so that they can clearly understand the answers to these questions:

What can be done at the center?

How is each activity, game, etc., used?

Where are the materials necessary for production kept?

Where are the finished products to be stored?

What do I do if I need help?

When can the center be used?

The introduction of a center can be provided:

as an overview of materials and activities presented to the whole class.

as a session for a small group of students, who then have the responsibility of training other students in using the center.

by daily teaching sessions (perhaps two activities per day).

by taped step-by-step directions.

by an aide or tutor who has been instructed on how to use the center.

on a day-to-day basis, supplying a center with only a few center activities at first, and adding one or two each day, or whenever students are ready.

The teacher should motivate and encourage students to use the learning center by doing the following:

adding new activities or materials to the center.

letting students create their own activities at the center.

having teacher-directed lessons in small or large groups at the center.

providing opportunities for sharing and teaching among the students who have worked at the center.

The teacher should provide some means for record keeping and evaluating so that both students and the teacher can account for time spent and learnings accomplished at the learning center.

The teacher should monitor the learning center, through observation and checking of record keeping systems, for the purpose of preventing problems or spotting problems that need solutions. The following is a brief sampling of possible problems and solutions, related to using learning centers.

Problems	Possible Solutions
students do the same activity over and over	design a sequence of assignments for the student(s)
students seem unable to follow activity directions	review directions—may need rewriting or more step-by-step format;
students resist using center	assign student helpers; replace less appealing activities; revitalize center with new activities, teacher-directed activity, etc.

VARIATIONS ON LEARNING CENTER MATERIALS AND ACTIVITIES

The learning centers in this book contain activities and materials designed, most often, by the teacher (or aide following the teacher's direction). Other alternatives for developing activities and supplying materials are:

commercially available materials and equipment.

textbooks.

child-created learning centers.

Centers Based on Commercial Materials

After determining the skills, content, or interest area of a learning center:

1. Go through and set aside related materials: your own, other teachers', the school's, the district resource center's, etc.

2. If the materials are not of a sufficient variety or range, supplement with materials ordered from catalogs and with some you make yourself.

3. After selecting the commercial materials you will use, renumber, retitle, and write directions that suit center needs.

4. Develop display and storage items that make the materials accessible to children who will use the center.

5. Develop record keeping and evaluation materials and a procedure for using them.

Centers Based on Textbooks

After determining the skills, content or interest area of a learning center:

1. Go through current textbooks (for your own grade as well as other grades) and mark applicable parts in some way, such as with bookmarks, paper clips, signs, and tabs.

2. Go through old textbooks and partially used workbooks (a good reason for a school to keep a supply of these) and cut out sections you will use for center activities.

3. Redo numbering, titles, and directions as needed.

4. Cut out from sources and laminate (use a machine or clear contact paper) individual pages or store in plastic envelopes or food-storage bags.

5. Supply any related realia or equipment.

6. Develop record keeping and evaluation materials and a procedure for using them.

THE CHILD-CREATED LEARNING CENTER

The major purpose of the child-created learning center is to provide additional opportunities for individuals to explore and create. The center also allows students to help structure the classroom environment, increases student participation in learning, and stimulates opportunities for student recognition. The child-created learning center provides student-to-student communication and exchange. Students can be responsible for creating a new center or adding to an existing one. Individual students may develop centers as an outgrowth of independent study. Centers may also be developed by small groups as an assigned task or because of a common interest.

Student Interests Catalog

Set up a notebook with a page for each child. Every other week or month each child is responsible for filling in his or her page in the catalog. At the end of each time span, several children are responsible for tabulating the information on the individual sheets into an Interest Index, which may be placed in the back of the catalog. Completed catalogs may be used in a variety of ways, such as by the teacher to plan new activities and centers, and by children who are planning centers to locate others who have similar interests. The catalog can also be useful in setting up groups, study pairs, and student tutors.

Coupon Book

Each coupon represents an ingredient in the learning center. A student selects a page in the coupon book, tears it out, and follows the directions on that page to add to his or her learning center.

Learning Center Model

Setting up a model for a learning center helps students visualize what components are necessary for their own learning centers. This model can serve as a reference for students throughout the year.

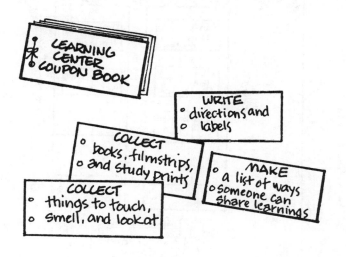

Announcements Pocket Chart

This chart announces happenings at the various child-created centers. It introduces students to new things at the centers and acts as a reminder for students to use in scheduling their own time.

ADD Chart

This chart gives recognition to students who will be contributing to the center. It reminds the students and the teacher of who has made a commitment to do an activity.

Open Bulletin Board

The students illustrate or write what they have learned at the center. As the board is filled, it becomes a mosaic of learnings.

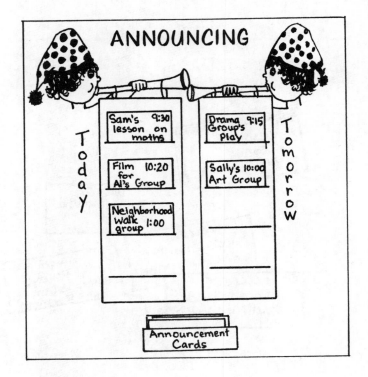

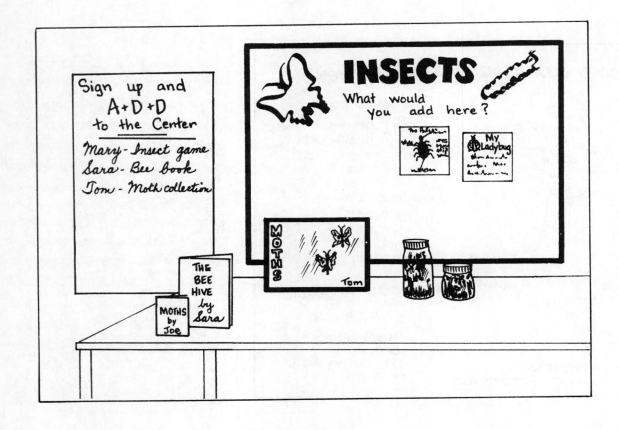

Child-Taught Lessons

To encourage sharing and to spark interest in a center, students can teach their classmates. Provide students with a guide to assist them in organizing and presenting their lessons. It will help to insure a high-quality lesson and success for the "teacher."

Center Evaluation

Students use this instrument to evaluate the learning center and give feedback to those who created the center. It also emphasizes the concept that learning centers belong to the class and, thus, can be modified according to class suggestions and needs.

HOW TO TEACH A LESSON AT YOUR CENTER

ANSWER THESE QUESTIONS BEFORE YOU TEACH

1. What do I want to teach?
2. How will I spark interest for my lesson?
3. What materials will I need to use?
4. What will my teaching steps be?
5. What will students do or make during or after the lesson?
6. How will I evaluate my lesson?

CENTER: _____

WHAT I LIKED TO DO BEST: _____

WHAT I LIKED TO DO LEAST: _____

WHAT I WOULD HAVE ADDED TO THE CENTER: _____

3
Ready-to-Use Learning Centers

AN INTRODUCTION TO LEARNING CENTERS

A learning center varies in its purpose just as it varies in its content and placement. Some centers direct students toward the learning of specific knowledge or skills. Some stress the development of thinking and learning processes. Other centers employ topics, techniques, and tools which capture the student's enthusiasm and entice him or her to participate in learning.

The contents of a learning center change according to the purpose and type of the center. Each center will have a different variety and quantity of activities: games, worksheets, and manipulative activities. In addition to the activities shown in each of the following centers, the teacher will need to supply such things as realia, books, and raw materials.

New centers can be created by selecting appropriate activities from several centers within this book and reorganizing them around a theme, topic, or skill area. An activity from one of the centers in this section can be adapted by using the activity's format with new vocabulary or other content appropriate to teacher or student needs.

The placement of a center changes according to its use. Some centers are displayed on tables while others can be stored in boxes and brought out periodically. The overviews of the learning centers in this section show a variety of ways and places to display center materials. Any of these display options (or others) may be selected by the teacher for any center, depending on available classroom space and organization.

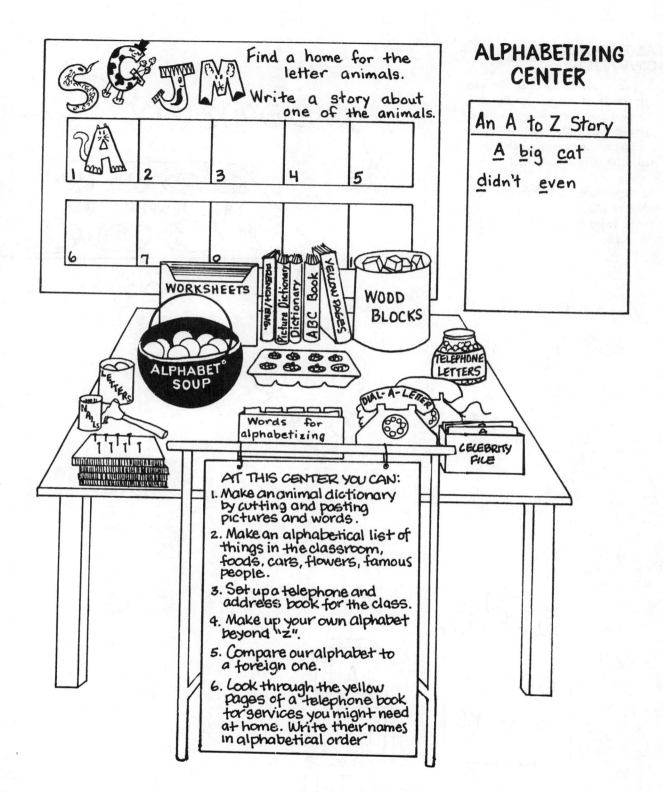

Find a home for the letter animals.

Write a story about one of the animals.

1	2	3	4	5
6	7			

ALPHABETIZING CENTER

An A to Z Story

A big cat didn't even

WORKSHEETS

Picture Dictionary · Dictionary · ABC Book · YELLOW PAGES

WODD BLOCKS

ALPHABET SOUP

LETTERS · NAILS

Words for alphabetizing

DIAL-A-LETTER

TELEPHONE LETTERS

CELEBRITY FILE

AT THIS CENTER YOU CAN:
1. Make an animal dictionary by cutting and pasting pictures and words.
2. Make an alphabetical list of things in the classroom, foods, cars, flowers, famous people.
3. Set up a telephone and address book for the class.
4. Make up your own alphabet beyond "z".
5. Compare our alphabet to a foreign one.
6. Look through the yellow pages of a telephone book for services you might need at home. Write their names in alphabetical order.

LEARNING POSSIBILITIES

Recognizing the names of letters
Learning the sequence of the alphabet
Learning to alphabetize
Developing ability to use various kinds of dictionaries

GAMES AND ACTIVITIES

1. Write letters on beads of various sizes and colors. A muffin tin or divided box may be used as the "jewelry box." Children use yarn or string to string beads in alphabetical order or to spell words.

2. Tape words and letters on small plain blocks. Children arrange letter or word blocks in alphabetical sequence.

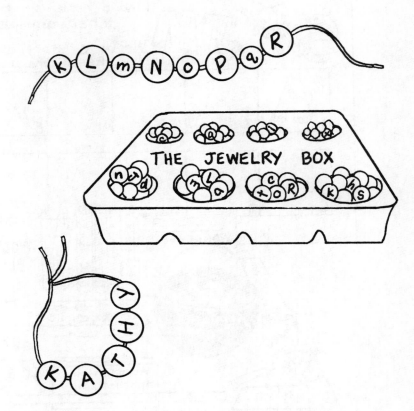

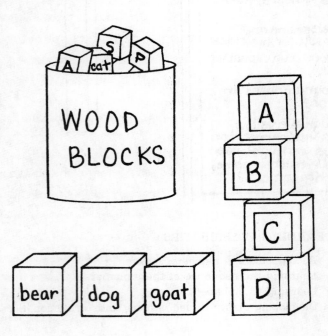

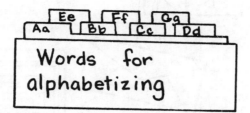

3. Place dividers for each letter of the alphabet in a box. Children add word cards to the box behind the appropriate divider.

Children remove all the cards from the box, shuffle, and re-alphabetize them.

4. Draw or paint several numbered circles on a board. Write words on paper circles and place them in a container. Children take several words, arrange them in alphabetical order, and nail or thumbtack them to the appropriate spaces on the board.

5. Write letters on paper circles or squares and place them in a cooking pot. Children ladle out letters and arrange them in alphabetical order.

6. Provide envelopes for each letter of the alphabet. Children cut out names of celebrities from magazines and newspapers and place them in the envelopes by the last name. A child selects six to ten names from an envelope and glues them to a sheet of paper in alphabetical order or to a worksheet such as the "billboard" pictured here. Phrases and pictures can be added to show how the celebrities might endorse or advertise an event or product.

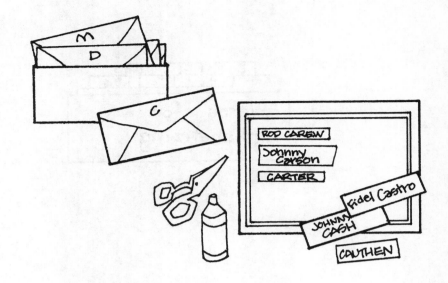

7. Draw telephones on heavy cardboard. Write letters or words on paper circles and put them in a container. Children select circles from the container and arrange them in alphabetical order on the telephone dial.

   Putting several cardboard telephones at the center makes it possible for children to play a game. The first child to alphabetize his or her letters or words correctly is the winner.

WORKSHEETS

Name_____ Date_____

SEND A TELEGRAM

Cut words from magazines and newspapers. Paste them in alphabetical order to make up a telegram to send to a friend.

TELEGRAM
_____
_____
_____
_____
_____
_____
_____
_____
_____
                              _____

Name_____ Date_____

HOW DOES YOUR GARDEN GROW?

Draw different petals around each flower. Cut and paste the flowers
to the stems in ABC order.

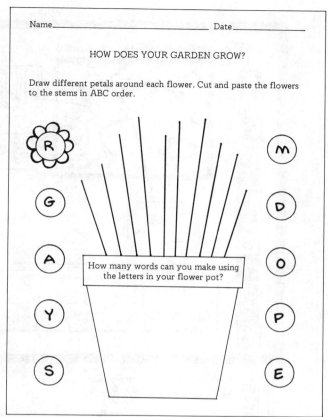

How many words can you make using
the letters in your flower pot?

FULL-SIZE WORKSHEET ON PAGE WS-1

Name_____ Date_____

Draw a picture of an object. List words
inside your picture that begin with the
same letter as the object and that are
related to the object in some way. Think
of: functions, parts, adjectives that describe
it, etc. Rewrite the words in alphabetical
order in the space provided.

EXAMPLE

fin
float
food
fish
flounder

1._____
2._____
3._____
4._____
5._____
6._____
7._____
8._____
9._____
10._____
11._____
12._____
13._____
14._____

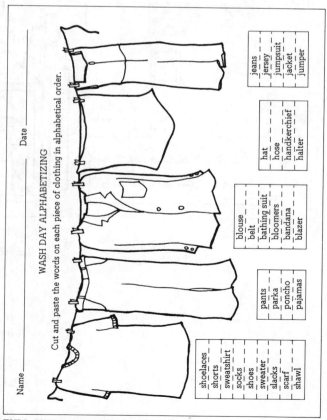

Name_____

Date_____

WASH DAY ALPHABETIZING

Cut and paste the words on each piece of clothing in alphabetical order.

jeans
jersey
jumpsuit
jacket
jumper

hat
hose
handkerchief
halter

blouse
belt
bathing suit
bloomers
bandana
blazer

pants
parka
poncho
pajamas

shoelaces
shorts
sweatshirt
socks
shoes
sweater
slacks
scarf
shawl

FULL-SIZE WORKSHEET ON PAGE WS-2

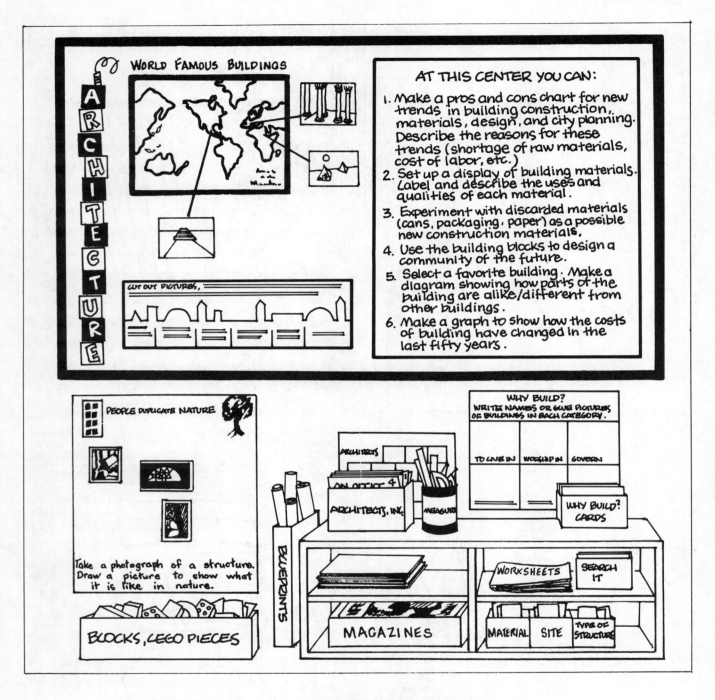

LEARNING POSSIBILITIES

Learning about famous architects and famous structures and their locations in the world

Learning about different styles and periods of architecture

Becoming aware of neighborhood buildings

Reinforcing the concepts that people adapt to their natural environment as well as change their environment to fit their needs

Learning about how and why things change by considering the past, present, and future

Using measuring instruments to make floor plans

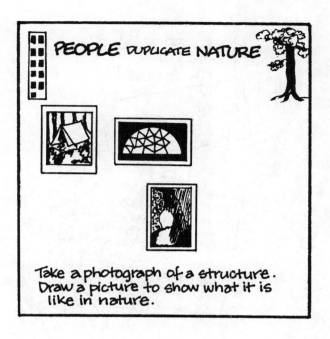

GAMES AND ACTIVITIES

1. Children take photographs of buildings which in some way duplicate or utilize nature in their construction. Then they make drawings to show the natural object, e.g., a bowl-shaped building duplicates a seashell.

2. Children research well-known buildings of the world and attach yarn to a drawing or picture of the structure to show their locations on a world map hung at the center. A time should be made available for children to share what they learned about the buildings.

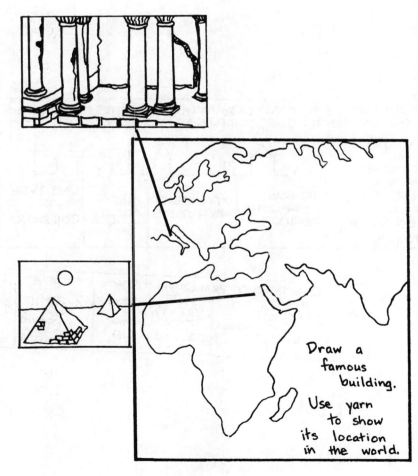

3. Make task cards that give clues or specifications for items that need to be included in a building design. Realtors' sheets describing homes, lots, and buildings for sale can also be used. Children incorporate task card items with their own ideas and draw a floor plan of the structure. Children may also want to make a model or rendering of the structure.

4. Make a large time-line activities chart. Provide children with long strips of paper on which to make their time lines. Students who have had little experience in making time lines will need some introductory teaching and practice time before they can independently complete this activity.

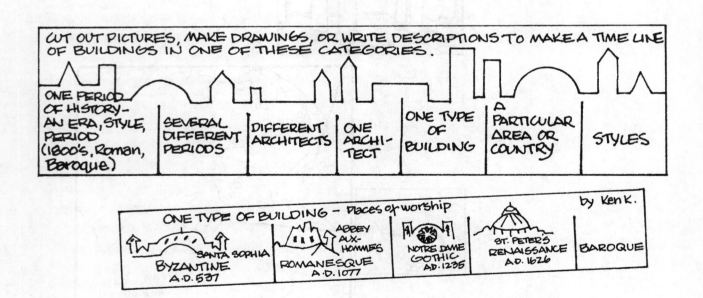

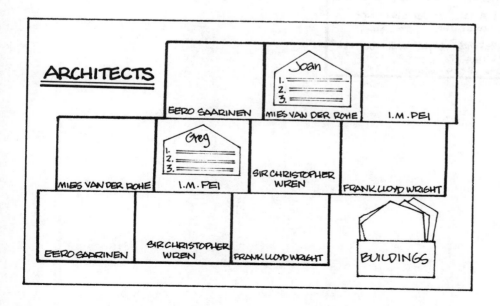

WHY BUILD?
WRITE NAMES OR GLUE PICTURES OF BUILDINGS IN EACH CATEGORY.

Monticello	*Notre Dame*
TO LIVE IN	TO WORSHIP IN
	U.N. Building
TO BE ENTERTAINED IN	TO GOVERN FROM
TO LEARN IN	TO WORK IN
TO GET HELP FROM	TO SHOP IN

WHICH HOME WAS DESIGNED BY A PRESIDENT OF THE U.S.?

BUILT IN 1950 BY A GROUP OF ARCHITECTS FROM MANY COUNTRIES

AN EXAMPLE OF GOTHIC ARCHITECTURE LOCATED ON AN ISLAND IN THE SEINE RIVER

5. Section off a large piece of paper and label each panel with a title. Children add names and pictures of structures that fit into each category.

When completed, the chart can be used as a means for discussing topics such as:

Why do people build?

How does the structure reflect the culture or environment?

Does form follow function?

When the chart has been completed, make a set of cards with questions or statements related to the buildings on the chart. Children select a card and place the card on the picture or name of the building that correctly answers the question or matches the description.

6. Make a gameboard with the names of architects in each square. Each architect's name should appear in several squares. Cut out small buildings or provide paper for children to cut out their own.

Children choose an architect and find out, through research, three facts about the architect or his or her buildings. These facts, along with the child's name, are written on one of the buildings and pinned above the architect's name. New facts must be found for other squares that contain the same architect's name. The child with the most buildings wins the game.

ARCHITECTS

	EERO SAARINEN	Joan 1. 2. 3. MIES VAN DER ROHE	I.M. PEI
MIES VAN DER ROHE	Greg 1. 2. 3. I.M. PEI	SIR CHRISTOPHER WREN	FRANK LLOYD WRIGHT
EERO SAARINEN	SIR CHRISTOPHER WREN	FRANK LLOYD WRIGHT	BUILDINGS

7. Make three sets of cards: UN-USUAL SITES, RAW MATERIALS, and TYPES OF STRUCTURES. Children choose one card from each category and build the structure in miniature on a simulated location.

8. Make task cards about housing or buildings in various geographical locations. Questions should pertain to the materials found in each area and how they affect what is built there.

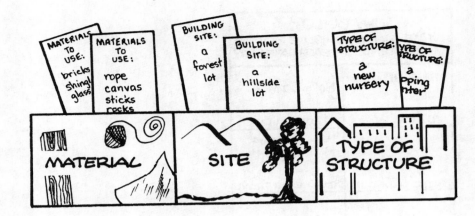

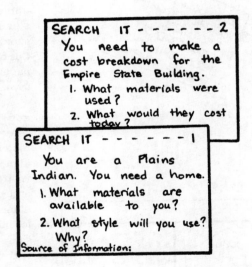

WORKSHEETS

Name_____ Date_____

FROM CAVE
TO
SKYSCRAPER

Show what changes
took place.

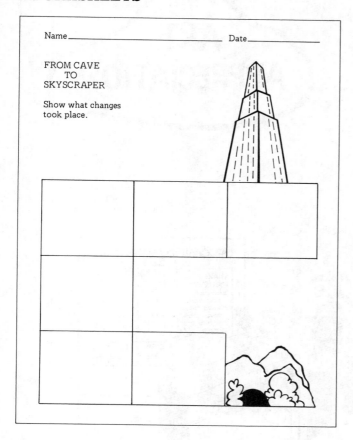

Name_____

Date_____

Observe and study the buildings in your neighborhood or city.
Complete the form below for buildings in each category.

	Date Built	Where Located	Bldg. Use Originally & Present	Outstanding Features	Architect	Materials	Design Appropriate to Surroundings	Rating	Recommendations
School									
Place of Worship									
Recreation									
Government									
Store									
Home									

FULL-SIZE WORKSHEET ON PAGE WS-3

Name_____

Date_____

What is your favorite style of architecture? Redesign the building in this style.

Answer these questions.

Address:

When built?

What is it used for?

What materials is it made of?

Describe the style of the building.

Make a sketch of one of your favorite buildings in your neighborhood or city.

Name_____ Date_____

Prepare a multiple choice test for a classmate to take. Questions might pertain to architecture vocabulary, famous architects, architect's tools, or a math problem to solve.

If the test taker successfully completes your test, present him with an Architect Tech diploma.

ARCHITECT'S TECH TEST

A B C D

1. ☐ ☐ ☐ ☐

2. ☐ ☐ ☐ ☐

3. ☐ ☐ ☐ ☐

4. ☐ ☐ ☐ ☐

5. ☐ ☐ ☐ ☐

6. ☐ ☐ ☐ ☐

7. ☐ ☐ ☐ ☐

8. ☐ ☐ ☐ ☐

- - - - - - - - - - - - - - - - - -

ARCHITECT'S TECH DIPLOMA

Having successfully completed the test designed by

_____
test maker

_____
test taker

is awarded this diploma on _____
date

FULL-SIZE WORKSHEET ON PAGE WS-4

AT THIS CENTER YOU CAN:

1. Make a portfolio or collection of your favorite works of art.
2. Remake a famous sculpture using junk.
3. Make a "mood display" of famous works of art which show quiet, calm, excitement, anger, etc.
4. Make a list of famous art museums and some of the well-known works displayed in each museum.
5. Compare a sculpture and a painting having the same theme. Does one portray the theme better? Tell why.
6. Make replicas of famous works of art for a Class Museum Gift Shop to sell. Reproductions can be in the form of greeting cards, note paper, posters, etc.

LEARNING POSSIBILITIES

Developing an appreciation of art and personal preferences
Recognizing various elements of art—line, texture, color, and form
Learning about different artists and styles of art
Experimenting with various media, techniques, and styles of art
Developing art vocabulary
Developing critical thinking, comparing and contrasting

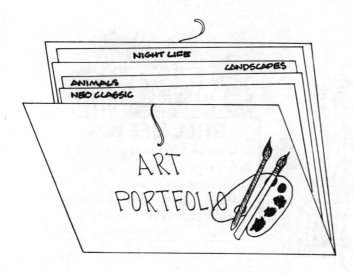

GAMES AND ACTIVITIES

1. Make a portfolio with two pieces of cardboard taped at the bottom. Cover with contact paper, and add string or ribbon to close the top. Children copy a famous painting or find a print of it and file it in the portfolio according to the topic headings.

2. Place copies of palettes at the art center. Children fill in each circle with information about the artist and his or her works.

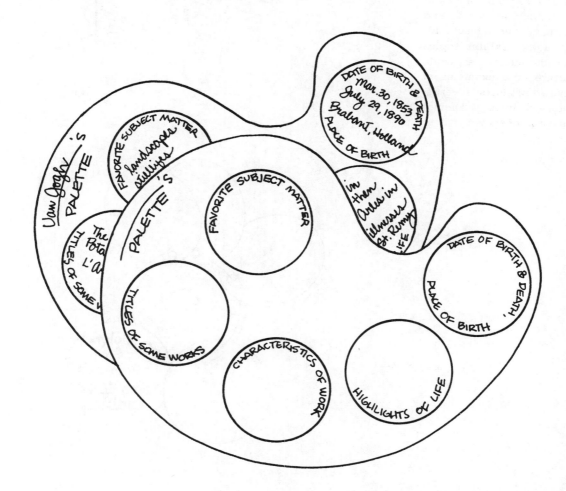

3. Collect materials such as a vase, artificial flowers, plastic fruit, branches, bottles, pieces of fabric, and bowls for the still-life box. Place art materials and tools (brayer, brushes, palette knife, fixative, charcoal, pastels, crayons, colored paper, acrylics, watercolors, clay, and linoleum or wood blocks) in another sturdy box—a utility box with compartments makes it easier to keep things organized. Children experiment first with the materials and tools and then set up a still life to use as the subject for their art work.

4. Children mix colors to match those in a print they have chosen. They paint each color on a circle of paper and hang all the circles together with the print.

5. Set up an area for exhibits and discussions. Children add to and maintain the area as subject matter is changed. Exhibit topics should include children's art work, art in nature, and examples of commercial art products (advertising, furniture, fashion, packaging) as well as works of known artists.

STILL LIFE BOX
1. Choose several objects.
2. Arrange them in an interesting way.
3. Use paint, chalk, crayons, or charcoal to draw your arrangement.

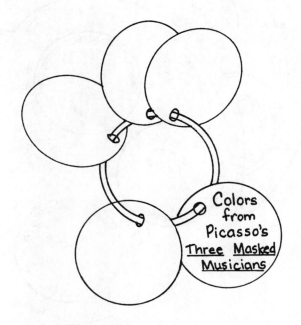

Colors from Picasso's Three Masked Musicians

6. Using empty boxes, children create their own art museum displaying their favorite works of art. A guide to their art museum describing the works and why they are favorites is written for other children to read as they "tour" the museum. The worksheet on page 46 can be used for guidebook pages.

7. Make an art museum out of empty boxes and prepare room labels with names of artists, styles, techniques, and subjects (Miro, Impressionism, pastels, portraits). Collect postcards and pictures for children to categorize. Children select a label for each room and classify pictures according to the room's name.

WORKSHEETS

Name_____ Date_____

1. Choose a painting.
2. Describe the painting by writing words, phrases, or sentences inside the frame.
3. See if someone else can guess which painting you have "framed."

FULL-SIZE WORKSHEET ON PAGE WS-5

Name_____ Date_____

Title of work:
Artist:
Medium:
Date of work:
Country work was executed in:
Interesting notes about the work or artist:

This is one of my favorite works because:

A Guide to

_____'s

Favorite Works

of Art

Name_____ Date_____

Write a Critic's Corner column that compares two works of art. In making your comparison think about artist's style, reason for work, medium used, when created, subject matter, mood of work and use of elements of art.

Critic's Corner

Title of work _____ DIFFERENCES _____
Artist _____
Medium _____
Date of Work _____

Title of work _____
Artist _____
Medium _____
Date of Work _____

SIMILARITIES _____ SUMMARY _____

FULL-SIZE WORKSHEET ON PAGE WS-6

Name _____

Date _____

OH SAY, CAN YOU SEE?

Choose a work of art and find out what people see in it. Take along a picture of the work you have chosen.
Title of work: _____

Artist's Name: _____

Interview these people. Write their names in the spaces.	Ask them these questions. "What do you think this work is about?" "What things or emotions do you see in the work?"	Do they like the work?		How much would they pay for it?
		Yes	No	
Someone under six years of age				
Someone your age				
A teenager				
Someone with glasses				
Someone with a mustache				
Someone who "towers" above you				
Someone wearing your favorite color				

FULL-SIZE WORKSHEET ON PAGE WS-7

Bilingual

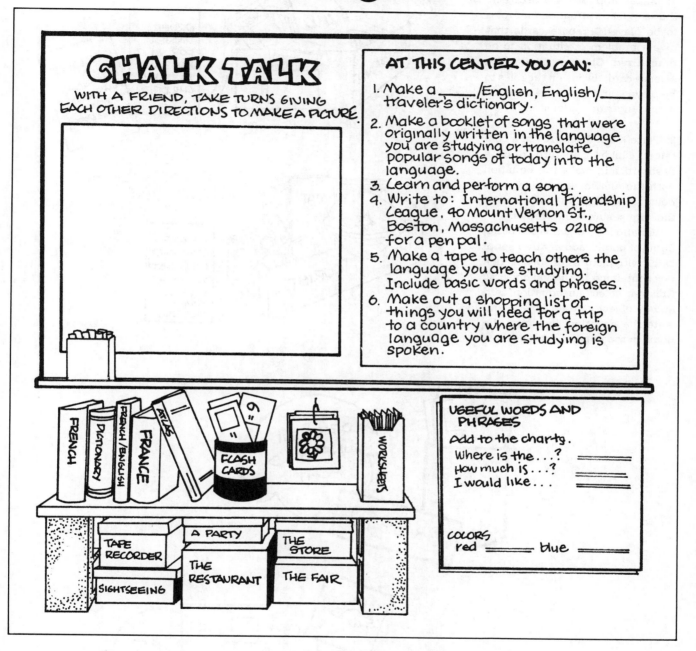

CHALK TALK

WITH A FRIEND, TAKE TURNS GIVING EACH OTHER DIRECTIONS TO MAKE A PICTURE.

AT THIS CENTER YOU CAN:

1. Make a _____/English, English/_____ traveler's dictionary.
2. Make a booklet of songs that were originally written in the language you are studying or translate popular songs of today into the language.
3. Learn and perform a song.
4. Write to: International Friendship League, 40 Mount Vernon St., Boston, Massachusetts 02108 for a pen pal.
5. Make a tape to teach others the language you are studying. Include basic words and phrases.
6. Make out a shopping list of things you will need for a trip to a country where the foreign language you are studying is spoken.

FRENCH · DICTIONARY · FRENCH/ENGLISH · FRANCE · ATLAS · FLASH CARDS · WORKSHEETS

TAPE RECORDER · A PARTY · THE STORE · THE RESTAURANT · THE FAIR · SIGHTSEEING

USEFUL WORDS AND PHRASES

Add to the charts.

Where is the...? =====
How much is...? =====
I would like... =====

COLORS
red _____ blue _____

LEARNING POSSIBILITIES

Developing and practicing a basic vocabulary and useful phrases

Learning about the customs, culture, and people of another country

Practicing conversation in another language

Reading and writing in a foreign language

Recognizing that our country has been influenced by the cultures and peoples of other countries

GAMES AND ACTIVITIES

1. Make "prop" boxes with objects that suggest a situation and roles to be played. Prepare cards that give a problem or situation to be dramatized. Children take a box, select a card, decide on the roles to be played, and enact the situation in the language under study.

2. Place math flashcards in a container. Children, in turn, draw a flashcard and state the equation with the answer in the language being studied. The person with the largest sum is the winner.

Variation: To practice the plural forms of nouns, add another set of cards with pictures of objects (or a box containing the actual objects). Children select an equation card and an object card (or object) and state the equation, including the noun, in the number sentence.

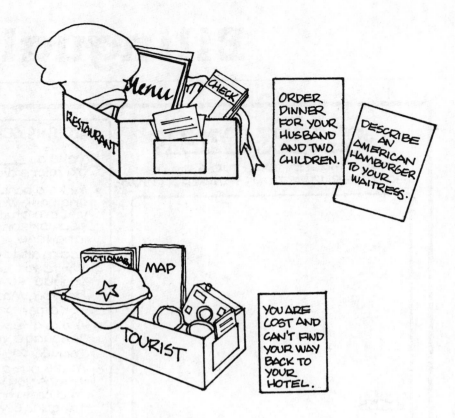

3. Write, in a foreign language, the names of places often used or visited. Hang these signs in various spots around the classroom. One child, the "visitor," asks another child, the "local," "Where is the ____?" or "How do I get to the ____?". The "local" gives directions for getting to the place (directions do not have to be the most direct route). The "visitor" follows the directions and is watched by the "local" to see if the directions were understood. Both children conduct their conversation in the language being studied.

Variation: Names of famous sites in the country where the language being studied is spoken can be substituted for place names.

4. Frame part of a chalkboard for children to use and provide them with colored chalk. Draw one part of a scene to use as a frame of reference—a window suggests a room; a tree, outdoors; a refrigerator, the kitchen; etc. Two or three children take turns giving each other directions, in the language under study, for adding objects to the scene. Encourage students to use words such as under, over, next to, below, and color words in their directions. When the picture is completed, the items in the scene can be labeled.

5. Getting to Know You—Using the format of the game show "What's My Line?," three children serve as panelists who ask questions in turn within a time limit. Three other children are guests who answer questions directed to them. The object of the game, however, differs from the original. The panelists, individually, must guess the *one* person *all* guests are impersonating. The guests and level of questioning will vary depending on the vocabulary the class has mastered.

Some guests might include:

a classmate,

a famous person whose first language is the language under study,

a celebrity,

a fictional person from literature.

WORKSHEETS

Name _____ Date _____

Language _____

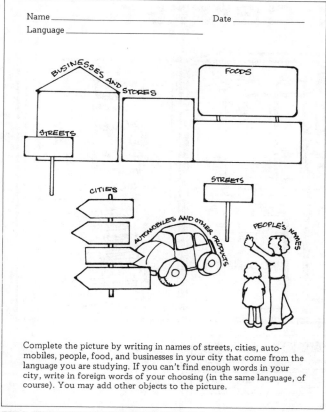

Complete the picture by writing in names of streets, cities, automobiles, people, food, and businesses in your city that come from the language you are studying. If you can't find enough words in your city, write in foreign words of your choosing (in the same language, of course). You may add other objects to the picture.

FULL-SIZE WORKSHEET ON PAGE WS-8

Name _____ Date _____

FOREIGN FACT FINDER

Select a famous person whose native language is the language you are studying. Fill out the form with information about this person. You might want to try it out with information on yourself first.

Name _____

Date of Birth _____

Country of Birth _____

Age _____

Present Place of Residence (Country) _____

Occupation _____

Early Life _____

_____

_____

_____

Notable Achievements _____

_____

_____

_____

_____

_____

_____

_____

Name _____

Date _____

Language _____

COMPLETE THE WORKSHEET IN THE LANGUAGE YOU ARE STUDYING

1. Write in words, the time shown on each clock.

2. Prepare the calendar by writing in the month and days of the week, and numbering the days for one week of the month.

3. Write in something you see someone doing during one of the times on the clocks for each day of the week.

Name _____ Date _____

FOREIGN FUNNIES

Finish each panel of the cartoon strip by drawing a setting or background, objects, animals or other people. Write dialogue for the cartoon in the language you are studying.

FULL-SIZE WORKSHEET ON PAGE WS-9

CONSUMER CENTER

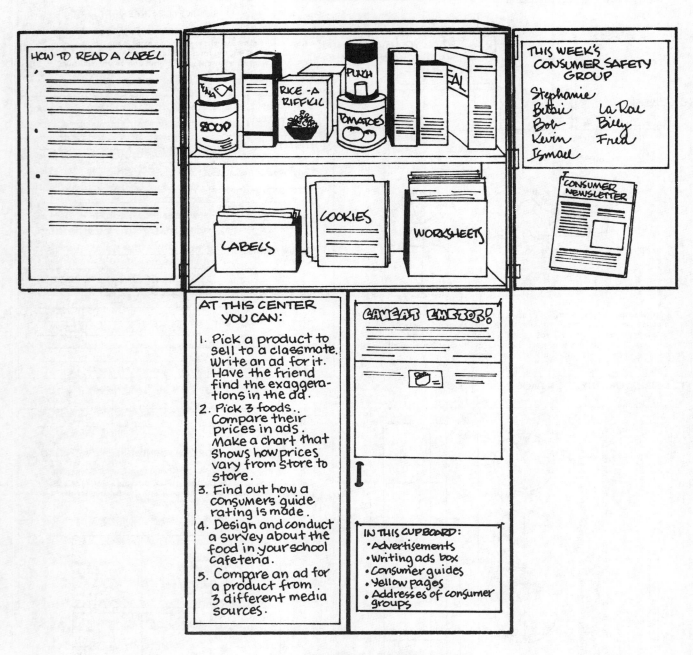

HOW TO READ A LABEL

THIS WEEK'S CONSUMER SAFETY GROUP

Stephanie
Bettie   La Rae
Bob   Billy
Kevin   Fred
Ismael

CONSUMER NEWSLETTER

AT THIS CENTER YOU CAN:

1. Pick a product to sell to a classmate. Write an ad for it. Have the friend find the exaggerations in the ad.
2. Pick 3 foods.. Compare their prices in ads. Make a chart that shows how prices vary from store to store.
3. Find out how a consumers' guide rating is made.
4. Design and conduct a survey about the food in your school cafeteria.
5. Compare an ad for a product from 3 different media sources.

CAVEAT EMPTOR!

IN THIS CUPBOARD:
- Advertisements
- Writing ads box
- Consumer guides
- Yellow pages
- Addresses of consumer groups

LEARNING POSSIBILITIES

Learning to be educated consumers
Understanding product labeling
Learning about comparative shopping
Working with a budget
Evaluating advertising

CAVEAT EMPTOR!

DOES AN AD TELL YOU EVERYTHING IN THE LARGE PRINT? READ THE SMALL PRINT, TOO, AND SEE.

LARGE PRINT — free poster

SMALL PRINT — need to have 3 cereal box tops

GAMES AND ACTIVITIES

1. Collect boxes of cereal or other products with ads on the back. Draw and hang the chart for children to complete.

2. Cut out the contents sections of labels from cans, boxes, or bags. Place them in envelopes labeled with types of food. Children may bring in more to replenish the envelopes. Make books to accompany each envelope, containing pages that list questions to be answered. Also, make and hang a chart instructing children how to read labels and what questions to ask themselves while reading them.

HOW TO READ A LABEL

- INGREDIENTS ON A LABEL ARE LISTED IN ORDER; THE INGREDIENT THAT MAKES UP THE BIGGEST PART OF THE PRODUCT IS LISTED FIRST.

- MANY LABELS LIST NUTRITIONAL INFORMATION FOR INDIVIDUAL SERVINGS.

- LOOK FOR A DATE ON THE LABEL. THIS TELLS YOU THE LAST RECOMMENDED DATE TO EAT OR USE A FOOD.

3. Help a small number of children form a consumer safety group. They will choose one or several products to evaluate, develop an evaluation form, survey their classmates and friends, and publish a newsletter containing information and recommendations relating to the products.

4. Paste eight pockets around the outside of a cardboard box. Label seven of these pockets with the following elements of a commercial: musical jingle, background music, well-known personality, factual information, slogan, humor, and other. Put blank cards in the eighth. Place products inside the box. Also make a kiosk or other similar arrangement for displaying finished commercials.

WORKSHEETS

Name_____ Date_____

ADVERTISE WISE

Name a product you have bought which you saw advertised.

_____

Where and when did you see the ad?_____

What did the advertisement promise you? _____

_____

Which part of the ad was accurate? _____

_____

Which part of the ad was not accurate?_____

_____

Would you buy the product again? _____

   Why or why not? _____

_____

What other products of its type would you be willing to buy?_____

_____

   Why?_____

_____

_____

_____

Name_____ Date_____

$$ CAN YOU BUDGET?

You get $10 allowance a month (4 weeks). You must buy lunch at school two times a week. Lunch costs 50¢. You also have to buy your school supplies. You may spend or save any money that is left.

Total $10 a month

Lunch   50¢ a time

       = _____ two times a week

       = _____ 4 weeks

Total lunch cost   _____

Money left after lunches   _____

School supplies for the month $2

Money left after expenses   _____

If you budget your money, how much extra will you have to spend or save each week?

How much each school day?   _____

How will you spend it? _____

Where will you spend it? _____

_____

_____

_____

FULL-SIZE WORKSHEET ON PAGE WS-10

Name_____ Date_____

BIG! EXAGGERATION BETTER!

Exaggeration is making something seem larger or greater than it really is. Sometimes manufacturers exaggerate when trying to sell their products. For example, a product advertised as a Giant Economy Size might be even more expensive per measure than another size.

Watch T.V. for one hour and answer these questions.

   How many commercials did you see?_____

   How many exaggerations did you hear or see?_____

List them. _____

_____

_____

_____

_____

_____

_____

_____

_____

_____

_____

_____

_____

Name_____ Date_____

PRICE PER MEASURE

Which do you think is the better buy? Figure out the price per measure to be sure.

	Check the one you think will be the better buy	Figure out and write in each products PPM
Clean-All Detergent 15 oz. box $1.50	☐	_____
Clean-All Giant Economy Size 30 oz. $3.00	☐	_____
Orange-O Orange Juice Concentrate 12 oz. makes ½ gallon $1.28	☐	_____
Fresh orange juice 1 quart $.96	☐	_____
Delicious Whole Wheat Bread 1 lb. loaf $1.12	☐	_____
Scrumptious Whole Wheat Bread 12 oz. Loaf $.96	☐	_____
See Through Window Cleaner 20 oz. bottle $1.00	☐	_____
See Through Trial Size 5 oz. bottle $.35	☐	_____
Moca-Coca 2 litre bottle $.75	☐	_____
Moca-Coca 6-pack (354 ml. per can) $1.50	☐	_____

FULL-SIZE WORKSHEET ON PAGE WS-11

COOKING CENTER

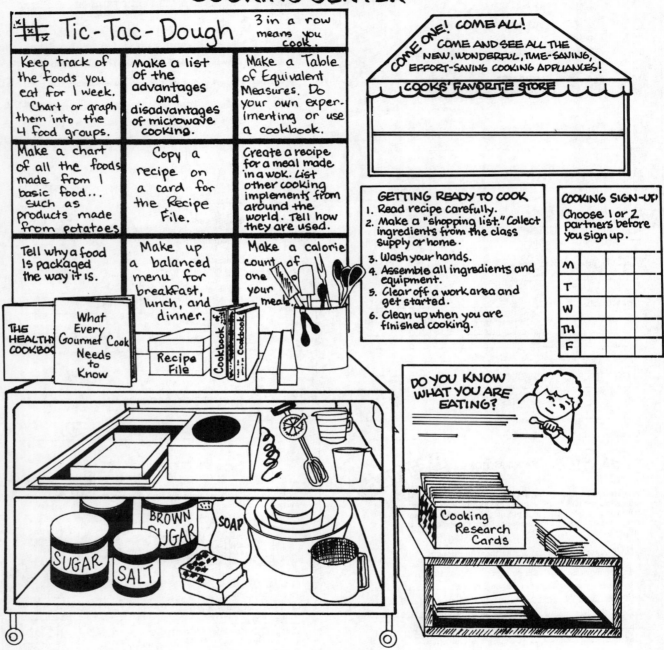

Tic-Tac-Dough
3 in a row means you cook.

Keep track of the foods you eat for 1 week. Chart or graph them into the 4 food groups.	Make a list of the advantages and disadvantages of microwave cooking.	Make a Table of Equivalent Measures. Do your own experimenting or use a cookbook.
Make a chart of all the foods made from 1 basic food... such as products made from potatoes	Copy a recipe on a card for the Recipe File.	Create a recipe for a meal made in a wok. List other cooking implements from around the world. Tell how they are used.
Tell why a food is packaged the way it is.	Make up a balanced menu for breakfast, lunch, and dinner.	Make a calorie count of one of your meals.

COME ONE! COME ALL! COME AND SEE ALL THE NEW, WONDERFUL, TIME-SAVING, EFFORT-SAVING COOKING APPLIANCES!

COOKS' FAVORITE STORE

GETTING READY TO COOK
1. Read recipe carefully.
2. Make a "shopping list." Collect ingredients from the class supply or home.
3. Wash your hands.
4. Assemble all ingredients and equipment.
5. Clear off a work area and get started.
6. Clean up when you are finished cooking.

COOKING SIGN-UP
Choose 1 or 2 partners before you sign up.

M			
T			
W			
TH			
F			

THE HEALTHY COOKBOOK

What Every Gourmet Cook Needs to Know

Recipe File

Cookbook

DO YOU KNOW WHAT YOU ARE EATING?

SUGAR

BROWN SUGAR

SALT

SOAP

Cooking Research Cards

LEARNING POSSIBILITIES

Learning about foods and nutrition

Learning planning and organizing through cooking

Developing ability to follow directions

Learning to use volume measurements

Working cooperatively with others

DO YOU KNOW WHAT YOU ARE EATING?

COMPARE THE INGREDIENTS IN A HOMEMADE RECIPE TO THOSE IN A STORE-BOUGHT PRODUCT.

HOMEMADE

macaroni
milk
cheese
salt

STORE-BOUGHT

MACARONI & CHEESE

macaroni
cheese
dry milk
artificial coloring
artificial flavoring

GAMES AND ACTIVITIES

1. Make available cookbooks and empty food containers. Post the chart for children to complete.

2. Put paper together to create a book. Children use cookbooks or their imaginations to put a traditional recipe or menu on the left and a more healthy substitute on the right.

THE HEALTHY BODY COOKBOOK

HOT FUDGE SUNDAE
vanilla ice cream
hot fudge sauce
whipped cream
nuts
cherry

YOGURT FRUIT SUNDAE
plain yogurt
fresh fruit
chopped nuts
sunflower seeds
spoonful maple syrup

3. This book contains two sections, *The ABC's of Cooking* and *Kitchen Hints*. Children add cooking terms and their definitions to the first section and helpful hints they have learned in cooking to the second section.

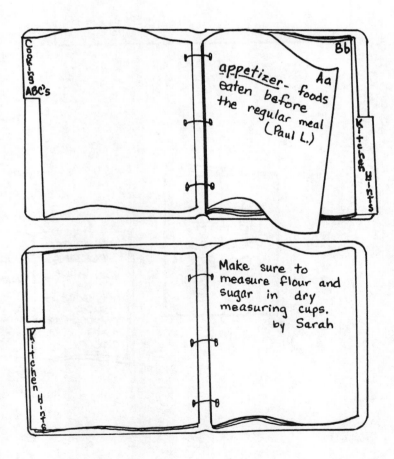

4. Children answer the questions on the research cards. They may also add a question to the research file.

5. Children make models of, draw, or cut out pictures of recently developed cooking appliances. Draw shelves inside the "storefront" for children to display their work.

WORKSHEETS

Name _____ Date _____

Sometimes recipes make more or less than you need. These recipes have to be changed to make the right amount for you.

Double this recipe of trail mix.

TRAIL MIX

150 g. nuts _____ g.
150 g. raisins _____ g.
100 g. sunflower seeds _____ g.
125 g. carob chips _____ g.

Halve this recipe for fruit salad.

FRUIT SALAD

700 g. grapes _____ g.
500 g. pineapple _____ g.
200 g. strawberries _____ g.
400 g. bananas _____ g.
Top with 300 g. yogurt _____ g.

Triple this recipe for yourself and eight friends to enjoy.

BANANA NOG

480 ml. cold milk _____ ml.
  2 eggs _____ eggs
15 ml. honey _____ ml.
  5 ml. vanilla _____ ml.
  1 large banana _____ bananas
Blend well.

FULL-SIZE WORKSHEET ON PAGE WS-12

Name _____ Date _____

INTERNATIONAL
FOOD MENU

Food	Country	Price
Sukiyaki	Japan	50 yen
Tacos.		
Paella.		
Crepes Suzette.		
Frankfurters		
Spaghetti.		

What can you add to this menu?

Name _____ Date _____

What foods are made in these ways?

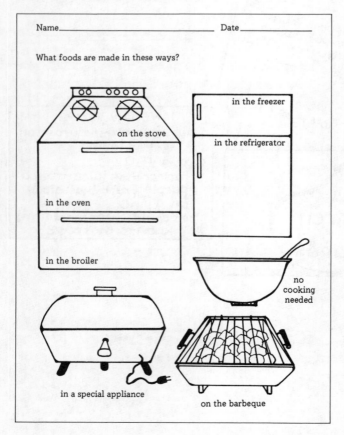

on the stove

in the freezer

in the refrigerator

in the oven

in the broiler

in a special appliance

on the barbeque

no cooking needed

Name _____ Date _____

DO YOU KNOW BASIC INGREDIENTS?

If you use the wrong kind of sugar, you might have gritty frosting. If you use the wrong kind of flour, your cake might feel like a rock. If you use a different kind of oil than your recipe calls for, your pancakes might taste like olives. Better find out the differences!

Kinds of Sugar	Description
_____	_____
_____	_____
_____	_____

Which is the best for you? _____ The worst? _____
Why? _____

Kinds of Flour	Description
_____	_____
_____	_____
_____	_____

Which is the best for you? _____ The worst? _____
Why? _____

Kinds of Oil	Description
_____	_____
_____	_____
_____	_____

Which is the best for you? _____ The worst? _____
Why? _____

Now write which kind of each ingredient would be best.

_____ sugar for frosting _____ flour for cakes
olive oil is good for _____

FULL-SIZE WORKSHEET ON PAGE WS-13

Cutting, Pasting, Folding, and Coloring

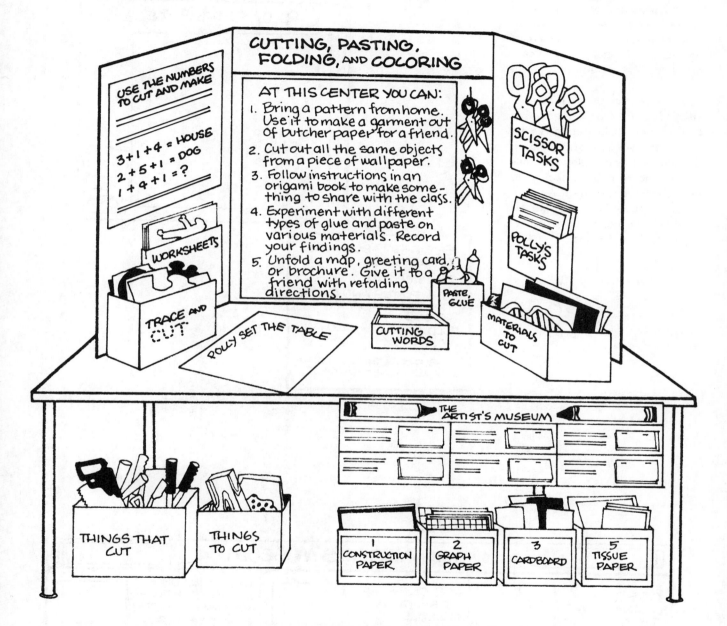

USE THE NUMBERS TO CUT AND MAKE

3 + 1 + 4 = HOUSE
2 + 5 + 1 = DOG
1 + 4 + 1 = ?

WORKSHEETS

TRACE AND CUT

POLLY SET THE TABLE

CUTTING, PASTING, FOLDING, AND COLORING

AT THIS CENTER YOU CAN:

1. Bring a pattern from home. Use it to make a garment out of butcher paper for a friend.
2. Cut out all the same objects from a piece of wallpaper.
3. Follow instructions in an origami book to make something to share with the class.
4. Experiment with different types of glue and paste on various materials. Record your findings.
5. Unfold a map, greeting card, or brochure. Give it to a friend with refolding directions.

SCISSOR TASKS

POLLY'S TASKS

PASTE, GLUE

CUTTING WORDS

MATERIALS TO CUT

THE ARTIST'S MUSEUM

THINGS THAT CUT

THINGS TO CUT

1 CONSTRUCTION PAPER
2 GRAPH PAPER
3 CARDBOARD
5 TISSUE PAPER

LEARNING POSSIBILITIES

Practicing the skills of cutting, pasting, folding, and coloring with a variety of materials and purposes

Using techniques of cutting, pasting, folding, and coloring in creative ways

Becoming independent in the use of scissors

GAMES AND ACTIVITIES

1. Children select a task card that directs them to perform a specific cutting, pasting, folding, and coloring task for setting the table. Directions for setting the table can be recorded for children who cannot read the task cards.

2. Each task in the Artist's Museum describes a different way to use crayons. Children can select or are assigned one of the tasks on the chart. They complete the task on the pad of paper attached to each frame on the chart. Another Artist's Museum chart can be made to serve as a place to display completed works of art.

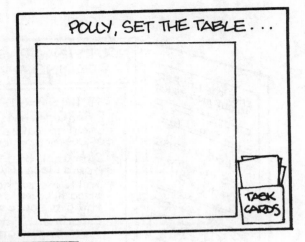

POLLY, SET THE TABLE . . .

TASK CARDS

SET THE TABLE FOR CHRISTMAS

You need to:

CUT 4 PLATES AND COLOR THEM IN CHRISTMAS COLORS.

FOLD NAPKINS INTO A △ SHAPE.

PASTE TOGETHER A SANTA CLAUS FOR THE TABLE.

JOIN THE ARTIST'S MUSEUM

USE 2 CRAYONS AT THE SAME TIME.

USE ONLY THE SIDES OF A CRAYON.

USE ONLY ONE COLOR. EXPERIMENT WITH DIFFERENT TEXTURES.

USE A LIGHT COLOR OVER A DARK COLOR.

USE ONLY THE POINTS OF A CRAYON.

USE EACH COLOR AT MAXIMUM BRILLIANCE.

USE THE NUMBERS
TO CUT AND MAKE

1 + 3 + 5 = HOUSE

2 + 5 + 3 = CAR

3 + 1 + 4 = DOG

2 + 5 + 4 + 1 = TREE

5 + 3 + 4 = SOMETHING
THAT FLIES

1 + 1 + 4 = ?

3 + 5 + 4 = ?

3. Sort various types of materials into boxes. Provide children with scissors and glue. The equations on the chart direct children to the types and amount of material needed to make a particular object.

4. Label each box and fill it with appropriate words, objects, or pictures of objects. Children are instructed to match items from two or three boxes.

1 CONSTRUCTION PAPER

2 GRAPH PAPER

3 CARDBOARD

4 FABRIC

5 TISSUE PAPER

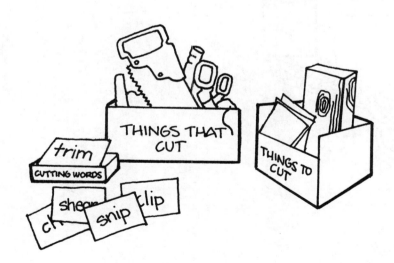

5. Draw and cut out different shapes from heavy cardboard to place in the container. Children trace around these patterns on paper and cut them out. These shapes can be decorated with scraps of different types of materials that are cut and pasted onto them.

6. Fill a box with different materials for children to cut. Make scissor-shaped task cards with various directions for cutting. Children select a task card and a material. They cut the material according to the directions written on the task card.

WORKSHEETS

Name_____ Date_____

SNIP AND STOP

Use one cut for each line segment. Stop where the sign is posted.

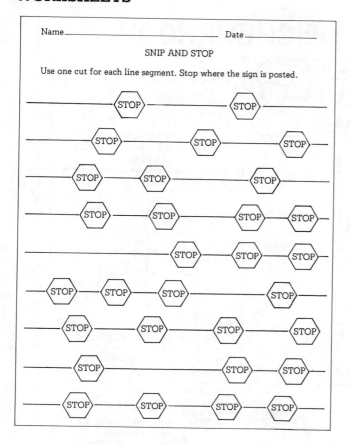

Name_____ Date_____

DOT — TO — DOT MONSTER CUT

Cut these lines between the numbers to make a monster.

1-2
3-4
5-6
7-8
9-10

11-12
13-14
15-16
17-18

DOT — TO — DOT MONSTER CUT

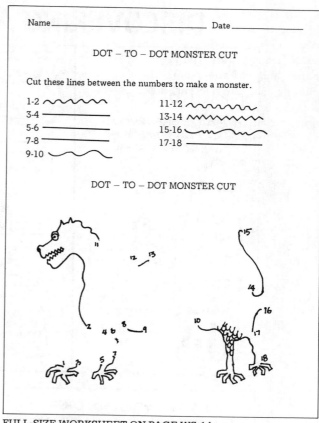

FULL-SIZE WORKSHEET ON PAGE WS-14

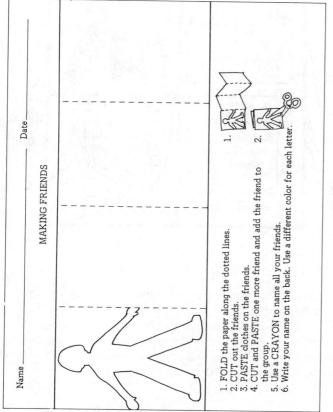

MAKING FRIENDS

Name_____

Date_____

1. FOLD the paper along the dotted lines.
2. CUT out the friends.
3. PASTE clothes on the friends.
4. CUT and PASTE one more friend and add the friend to the group.
5. Use a CRAYON to name all your friends.
6. Write your name on the back. Use a different color for each letter.

FULL-SIZE WORKSHEET ON PAGE WS-15

Name_____ Date_____

HARD-TO-CUT-OUTS

Cut out the third circle.

Cut around the snowflake.

Cut the board out of man's hand.

Cut the fruit out of the basket.

FULL-SIZE WORKSHEET ON PAGE WS-16

DISCOVERING A NEIGHBORHOOD

ALL IN A NEIGHBORHOOD

Take a NEIGHBORHOOD WALK. Add something from your walk to this board.

TRASH WALK

MY BIRD WALK

Colors of Houses

Neighborhood Interviews

Sam S., gardener

CLARA'S CLEANERS
Clara Smith, proprietor

WANTED for the NEIGHBORHOOD

Make a WANTED NOTICE for something needed in your neighborhood.

WANTED A bicycle rack for the vacant lot.

WANTED A new style telephone pole

Choose a WANT AD from this board. Design something or some way to "fill" the ad.

AT THIS CENTER YOU CAN:

1. Compare commercial and recreational places in your neighborhood to dwellings.
2. Make a graph of something in the neighborhood (houses, trees, house numbers, etc.).
3. Be a neighborhood surveyor. Collect measurements such as: heights of trees, lengths of driveways.
4. Write a neighborhood history by interviewing, reading old newspapers, and/or visiting the planning department.
5. Describe a family and design an apartment house, condominium, and a trailer that meets its needs.
6. Make a "CHANGING FACES- CHANGING PLACES" chart to record change in your neighborhood.

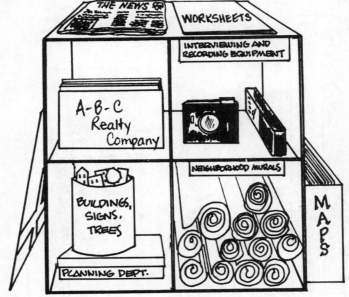

LEARNING POSSIBILITIES

Developing an awareness and involvement in one's own neighborhood

Developing the ability to be a careful observer

Learning about how people affect the nature of a neighborhood

Exploring alternatives for effecting change in a neighborhood

Applying measurement and map skills

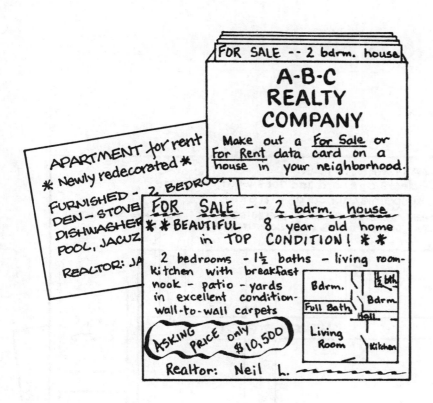

GAMES AND ACTIVITIES

1. Make a Realty Company box containing large, blank index cards. After taking a walk in the neighborhood, children write out data cards. They should include a drawing of the front of the building or a floor plan. Children may gather the information from observations of the building or from talking to people who live in it.

2. After a group walk, a student may make his own mural of part of the neighborhood. Using butcher paper, he may include three or four buildings, an entire block, a shopping center, or whatever else he wants. He may concentrate on some aspect studied by the class or on a specialized interest, such as plants, measurements, or building styles.

3. The teacher designs a game-board showing blocks, streets, and a directional indicator and toy buildings, signs, trees, etc., for use on the board.

The cards and board may be used several ways: as a small-group lesson with the teacher; as an individual, independent activity; or as a small-group competitive game.

To use as a competitive game, cards may carry points, depending on difficulty. Each player decides to try a more difficult or an easier card. He follows the directions and keeps the card. When the game is finished, a completed map (made by the teacher to fit the cards) is used to decide which players earn points.

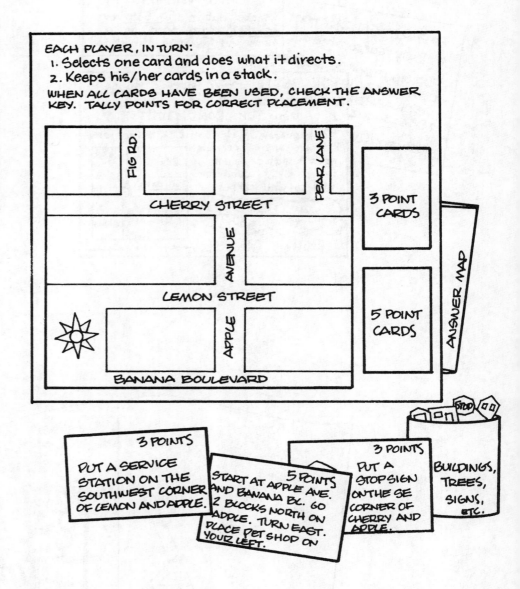

EACH PLAYER, IN TURN:
1. Selects one card and does what it directs.
2. Keeps his/her cards in a stack.

WHEN ALL CARDS HAVE BEEN USED, CHECK THE ANSWER KEY. TALLY POINTS FOR CORRECT PLACEMENT.

FIG RD.

PEAR LANE

CHERRY STREET

AVENUE

LEMON STREET

APPLE

BANANA BOULEVARD

3 POINT CARDS

5 POINT CARDS

ANSWER MAP

3 POINTS
PUT A SERVICE STATION ON THE SOUTHWEST CORNER OF LEMON AND APPLE.

5 POINTS
START AT APPLE AVE. AND BANANA BL. GO 2 BLOCKS NORTH ON APPLE. TURN EAST. PLACE PET SHOP ON YOUR LEFT.

3 POINTS
PUT A STOP SIGN ON THE SE CORNER OF CHERRY AND APPLE.

BUILDINGS, TREES, SIGNS, ETC.

4. Various kinds of recording equipment may be used in a variety of ways on walks: to describe or measure a house, building, or yard; to tape walking directions to a certain location, which may be tested out by another child; to interview neighbors, storekeepers, or community helpers; to record neighborhood sounds in various locations; to tape children's comments as they view a specific object (newly poured cement, a mailbox, a beehive); to record change in a building project; to tally counts of shrubbery and other objects, etc.

5. Planning Department—With children's assistance, mark a city or area map to show how it is zoned and regulated by laws or codes. Make a legend for the map. Ask the city or county Planning Department or the Building and Safety Department for help, if necessary.

Children write problems and questions related to their own or others' homes and businesses. Then they (or other children) place the cards on the map in appropriate locations.

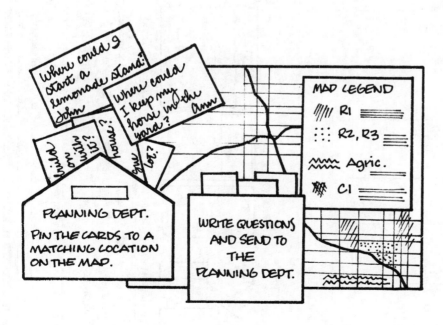

WORKSHEETS

Name _____ Date _____

Design a new house or apartment using elements from those around you. Choose each feature from a different house or apartment in your neighborhood.

Design a Home

Features you may wish to include:

door	walkway	steps
porch	T.V. antenna	chimney
mail box	windows	stairway
		balcony

Name _____ Date _____

Choose one building to look at. Categorize all of the items at the location (a home, an apartment, a store, a yard, a church) by listing them under the following headings.

Made of Wood

Growing Things

Made of Cement,
Brick, Plaster

Containing or
Made of Glass

Made of Metal

Made of Plastic

FULL-SIZE WORKSHEET ON PAGE WS-17

Name _____ Date _____

ALIKE = and ≠ DIFFERENT

Choose 6 buildings on a block. Use words or drawings to compare one feature of the houses, such as T.V. antennas, doors, windows, roofs or shrubbery. Look for things that are alike and different.

A NEIGHBORHOOD WALK

Name _____ Date _____

List kinds of stores & services

List city provided conveniences

MAIL

List kinds of signs

List the things you see in and around your neighborhood on the matching pictures. Go back and mark each thing in your lists using the following symbols:

◆ needs repairs
★ in good condition
☼ pleasing to look at
✳ useful to kids
☐ useful to animals
○ useful to adults

FILL IN THE FOLLOWING:

It is _____ _____ from my home to the nearest market.
(how many?) (steps, feet, meters)

It is _____ to the nearest gas station.
It is _____ to the nearest mail box.
It is _____ to the nearest park.

FULL-SIZE WORKSHEET ON PAGE WS-18

ECOLOGY

THE BASIC UNIT OF ECOLOGY:
ECOSYSTEMS

ENERGY SOURCE — SUN

PRIMARY PRODUCERS — PLANTS, GRASS

PRIMARY CONSUMERS — DEER MOOSE

DECOMPOSERS — BACTERIA IN SOIL

SECONDARY CONSUMERS — WOLF

AT THIS CENTER YOU CAN:

1. Make a diagram of the sciences that are related to ecology.

2. Write a script of an ecologist "talking" to a primary consumer.

3. Design anti-pollution posters for your neighborhood.

SOME ECOSYSTEMS

alpine meadow
your backyard
schoolyard
tidal flat
river delta
tidepool
fish pond

prairie
desert
meadow

lake
stream
pond
park

ATLAS · TREES · THE OCEANS · ECOLOGY · THE RED DATA BK · SIERRA CLUB

ECO WORD CHAIN STRIPS

ECOLOGY MATH LAB
1. _____
2. _____
3. _____

WORKSHEETS

MAPS

ECOSYSTEM MODELS SUPPLIES

COMPLETED ECOSYSTEMS

TIDEPOOL   SOIL

DESERT ECOSYSTEM

ECOLOGY PYRAMIDS
1. _____
2. _____
3. _____
4. _____
5. _____

BLOC

LEARNING POSSIBILITIES

Learning about and replicating ecosystems
Integrating and practicing math skills
Sequencing
Vocabulary development
Generating problems and solutions

GAMES AND ACTIVITIES

1. Ecology Math Lab—Set up an Ecology Math Lab that contains: number fact cards, (eco-facts) supplies for making problem cards, and paper and counting and measuring instruments for solving problems. Children choose one or more fact cards and make up three math problems based on them. They solve the problems and put the answers on the back. Other children try to solve problem cards left at the Lab by their classmates.

2. Ecological Pyramids*—Set up a collection of blocks and empty cartons and boxes. A child does research to learn about a food chain pyramid, builds a model of it, labels the parts, and reproduces it on paper. (If it is made of used boxes, etc., the pyramid model can be on permanent display and the other work can be shown on it.)

A "What Would Happen?" card is selected and the child writes problems that may arise if the situation occurs, and then proposes solutions for the potential problems.

*The basic idea of an ecological pyramid is that, due to energy loss, the volume of food at each level of a food chain is smaller than the volume at a previous level.

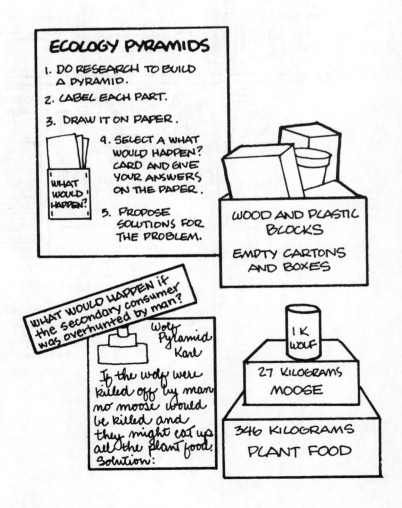

3. Ecosystem Models—Make the two charts: ECOSYSTEM RE-QUIREMENTS and EACH FOOD CHAIN MUST SHOW. Provide a supply of real objects (rocks, sand, shells, twigs, etc.), paper materials (Saran, foil, construction paper, etc.), strips for Food Chains, and cut-outs for Trouble Spots.

Children follow the directions on the charts and create a model of an ecosystem (see Overview for examples of ecosystems). The food chains they make can be attached to the box or tray that houses the ecosystem.

ECOSYSTEM REQUIREMENTS

1. SHOW LIVING AND NON-LIVING ELEMENTS.

2. LABEL THE PARTS OF ONE FOOD CHAIN.

3. MAKE 2 OTHER COLOR-CODED FOOD CHAINS OUT OF THE STRIPS AND ATTACH TO MODEL.

4. SHOW 3-5 TROUBLE SPOTS - PLACES OR THINGS PEOPLE HAVE DESTROYED OR ARE LIKELY TO HARM.

EACH FOOD CHAIN MUST SHOW...

PRIMARY PRODUCERS - plants, greens, that photosynthesize solar energy to become food

PRIMARY CONSUMERS - large or small organisms that eat the food

SECONDARY (POSSIBLY TERTIARY) CONSUMERS - animals that eat primary consumers for food

DECOMPOSERS - bacteria and fungi that break down plant and animal parts and wastes and return it to primary producers to be used again

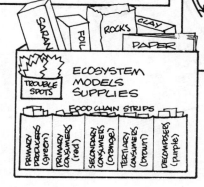

ECOSYSTEM MODELS SUPPLIES

TROUBLE SPOTS

SARAN FOIL ROCKS CLAY PAPER

FOOD CHAIN STRIPS

PRIMARY PRODUCERS (green) PRIMARY CONSUMERS (red) SECONDARY CONSUMERS (orange) TERTIARY CONSUMERS (brown) DECOMPOSERS (purple)

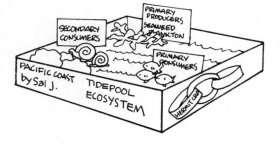

PACIFIC COAST by Sal J. TIDEPOOL ECOSYSTEM

SECONDARY CONSUMERS

PRIMARY PRODUCERS SEAWEED PLANKTON

PRIMARY CONSUMERS

HERMIT CRAB

4. Eco-word Chains—Provide a supply of paper strips of varying lengths, measured off into two-inch squares (or cut strips from commercial one-inch graph paper). Children write ecology-related words on the strips, horizontally or vertically, one letter to a square. They put the meanings of the words on the back, and store the strips in an envelope.

Other children use several of these strips to design a chain of eco-words and pin it up for display. They may wish to transfer their design to graph paper and make up a crossword for others to complete.

A game can be played with the word strips in which the strips are stacked and players, in turn, draw one and try to fit it onto another word strip, crossword puzzle fashion. If a word cannot be made to fit, it is returned to the stack. A graph can be kept of the number of words each group of players uses, and the winning group can be the one that uses the most.

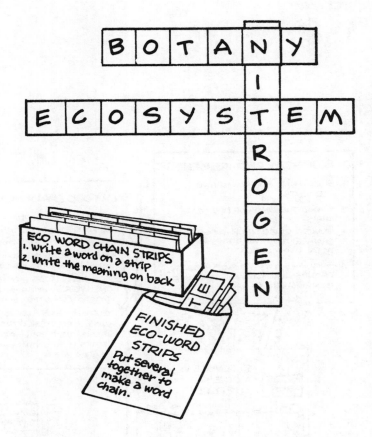

WORKSHEETS

Name _____ Date _____

POLLUTION – AN ECOLOGICAL PROBLEM
"Ecology Apologies"

1. Write one cause for each type of pollution.
2. Tell how one thing is affected by each type of pollution.
3. For each kind of pollution, write two "ecology apologies": things people say to try to make up for what we've lost or are losing.

A CAUSE: Nuclear wastes are buried in the ground.

A CAUSE:

AN EFFECT: People exposed to radioactivity have a greater chance of getting cancer.

AN EFFECT:

APOLOGIES:
1. It costs a lot to get rid of wastes. Do you want to pay for it? _____

1. _____
_____
_____

2. _____

2. _____

A CAUSE:

A CAUSE:

AN EFFECT:

AN EFFECT:

APOLOGIES:
1. _____

APOLOGIES:
1. _____

2. _____

2. _____

A CAUSE:

A CAUSE:

AN EFFECT:

AN EFFECT:

APOLOGIES:
1. _____

APOLOGIES:
1. _____

2. _____

2. _____

FULL-SIZE WORKSHEET ON PAGE WS-19

Name _____ Date _____

ENVIRONMENTAL NUMBER FACTS

<u>POPULATION NUMBER FACTS</u> Show the following facts in graph form.

1. About 74,000,000,000 persons have lived on the earth in the last 600,000 years.
2. The world population in 1970 was about 3,600,000,000. By the year 2000 it will be about 6,500,000,000.
3. The U.S. population in 1776 was about 4,000,000. In 1976, it was about 228,000,000. The U.S. population in 1970 was about 205,000,000. By the year 2040 it will probably double, to about 410,000,000.

<u>PERSONAL</u> and <u>PRODUCTION NUMBER FACTS</u> Chart the following information (except no. 5 and no. 6) in metric measurements.

1. Each person in the U.S. uses almost 60 gallons of water each day.
2. Each person in the U.S. uses almost 19 gallons of water each day for bathing.
3. A U.S. family of four eats about 260 pounds of pork each year.
4. Each Canadian eats about 96 pounds of beef each year.
5. Each American throws away about 5 pounds of rubbish daily.
6. Each car in the U.S. burns about 306 gallons of gas every year.
7. It takes about 17 trees to make 1 ton of newsprint.
8. About 48 acres of land must be cleared to build 1 mile of super-highway.
9. Oil refineries use about 500 gallons of water to produce 1 gallon of gas.
10. Paper companies use about 50 gallons of water to make 1 pound of paperboard.

FULL-SIZE WORKSHEET ON PAGE WS-20

Name _____ Date _____

CONSERVATION – AN ECOLOGICAL TASK

Write two questions you would like to ask each of the groups listed below.

1. World Wildlife Fund
   Suite 728
   910 17th St. N.W.
   Washington, D.C. 20036

My questions: □
   1. _____
   _____
   2. _____
   _____

2. ICCN (International Union for the Conservation of Nature)
   1110 Morges
   Switzerland

My questions:
   1. _____
   _____
   2. _____
   _____

3. National Wildlife Federation
   Dept. FB
   1412 16th Street, N.W.
   Washington, D.C. 20036

My questions:
   1. _____
   _____
   2. _____
   _____

4. Whale Protection Fund
   Center for Environmental
      Education, Inc.
   1925 K Street, N.W., Suite 206
   Washington D.C. 20006

My questions:
   1. _____
   _____
   2. _____
   _____

Write a letter to one of the groups (or to one you know about). Ask your questions and ask for any information or material they have available.

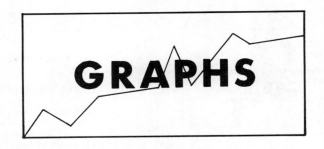

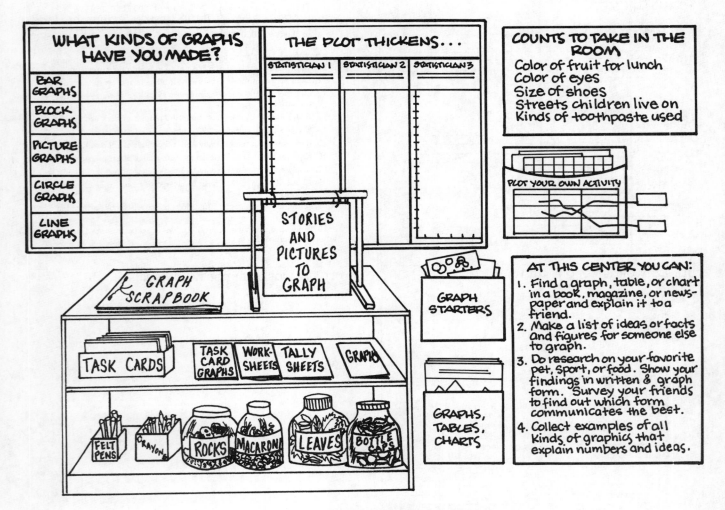

LEARNING POSSIBILITIES

Using graphs, tables, and charts as a form of communication
Recognizing the uses and purposes of graphs, tables, and charts
Making graphs, tables, and charts
Interpreting graphs, tables, and charts

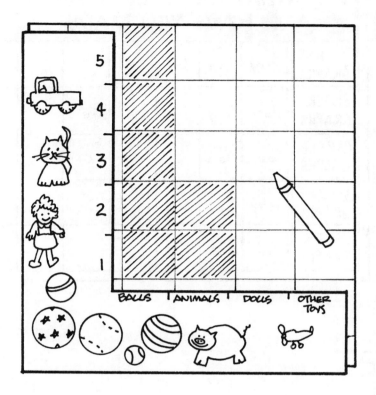

GAMES AND ACTIVITIES

1. Make a set of graph starters from right angles cut out of heavy paper. Put pictures or information to be graphed on the starter. Label each axis along the interior edge of the angle, depending on what is to be graphed. Children select a graph starter, copy the labels along each axis onto graph paper, and make a graph of the information shown visually or verbally on the starter.

2. Three children work at the chart at the same time. After reading the same specifically prepared story, each child shows the statistical information from the story in their table. Students compare their statistics and evaluate how their table communicates these statistics.

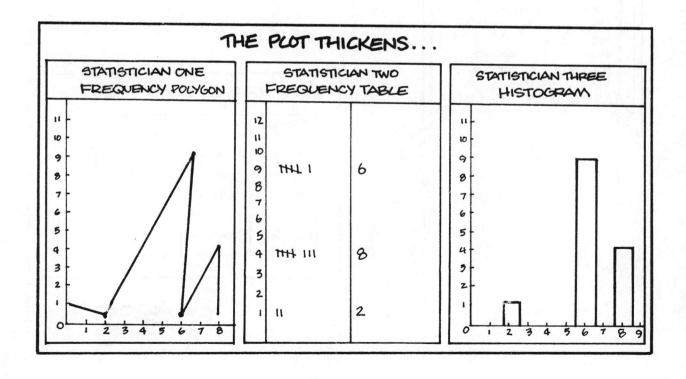

3. Use this chart to stimulate interest in making different types of graphs and to record the types of graphs children have developed.

4. Display stories and pictures containing number situations that may be graphed by children. Small groups of children can work with the teacher to create the stories for their classmates to graph.

5. Children design their own learning experience by selecting a purpose for graphing, a category to graph, and the type of graph to make. A piece of string is connected to each part of the activity to indicate the task the student will perform.

WHAT KINDS OF GRAPHS HAVE YOU MADE?

PICTURE GRAPHS	Terry	Jane	José			
BLOCK GRAPHS	Mary	Sally	Tom	Paul	José	
CIRCLE GRAPHS	Sally	Tom				
BAR GRAPHS	Terry	Paul	José			
LINE GRAPHS	Tom	Lisa				

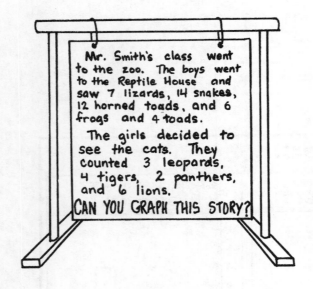

Mr. Smith's class went to the zoo. The boys went to the Reptile House and saw 7 lizards, 14 snakes, 12 horned toads, and 6 frogs and 4 toads.

The girls decided to see the cats. They counted 3 leopards, 4 tigers, 2 panthers, and 6 lions.

CAN YOU GRAPH THIS STORY?

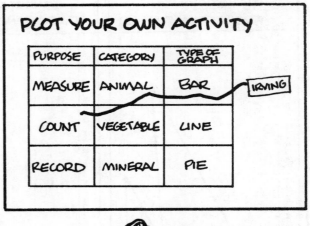

PLOT YOUR OWN ACTIVITY

PURPOSE	CATEGORY	TYPE OF GRAPH
MEASURE	ANIMAL	BAR
COUNT	VEGETABLE	LINE
RECORD	MINERAL	PIE

IRVING

6. Collect or make a variety of graphs, tables, and charts and place them in an envelope. Instruct children on how to use the worksheet that accompanies the materials in the envelope.

SPINACH	ENJOY	DISLIKE
BOYS	6	21
GIRLS	14	23
MEN	32	5
WOMEN	26	11

HAMBURGER SALES
—— MAC DANIELS
- - - JOHN-IN-THE-BOX

SALES IN 1000s

70 60 50 40 30 20 10

JAN FEB MAR APR MAY

GRAPHS, TABLES, AND CHARTS

NAME _____
DATE _____
TITLE OF GRAPH, TABLE, OR CHART _____
_____
WRITE A QUESTION NOT ANSWERED BY THE GRAPH, TABLE, OR CHART _____
_____
_____
RESEARCH YOUR QUESTION AND SHOW YOUR FINDINGS ON THE BACK OF THIS SHEET IN A NEW GRAPH, TABLE, OR CHART.

WORKSHEETS

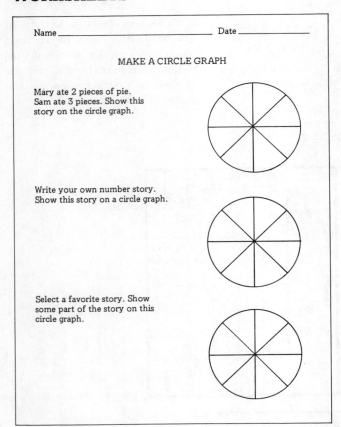

Name _____ Date _____

MAKE A CIRCLE GRAPH

Mary ate 2 pieces of pie. Sam ate 3 pieces. Show this story on the circle graph.

Write your own number story. Show this story on a circle graph.

Select a favorite story. Show some part of the story on this circle graph.

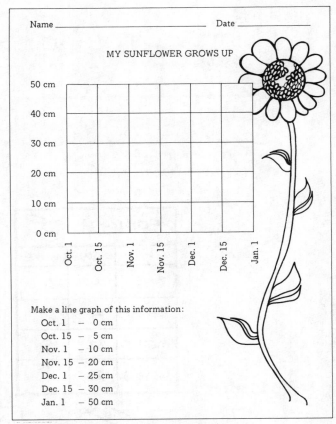

Name _____ Date _____

MY SUNFLOWER GROWS UP

Make a line graph of this information:

Oct. 1 — 0 cm
Oct. 15 — 5 cm
Nov. 1 — 10 cm
Nov. 15 — 20 cm
Dec. 1 — 25 cm
Dec. 15 — 30 cm
Jan. 1 — 50 cm

FULL-SIZE WORKSHEET ON PAGE WS-21

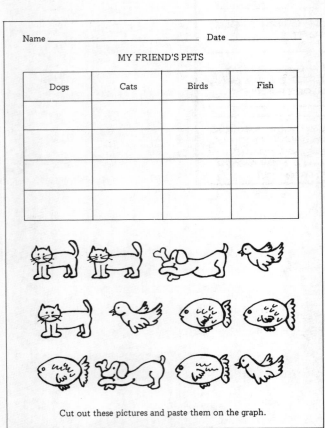

Name _____ Date _____

MY FRIEND'S PETS

Dogs	Cats	Birds	Fish

Cut out these pictures and paste them on the graph.

FULL-SIZE WORKSHEET ON PAGE WS-22

Health

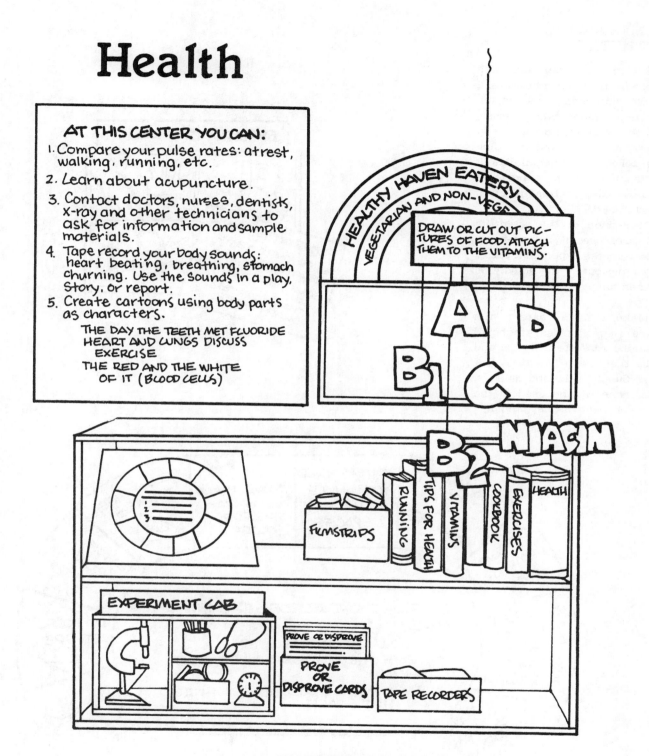

AT THIS CENTER YOU CAN:

1. Compare your pulse rates: at rest, walking, running, etc.
2. Learn about acupuncture.
3. Contact doctors, nurses, dentists, X-ray and other technicians to ask for information and sample materials.
4. Tape record your body sounds: heart beating, breathing, stomach churning. Use the sounds in a play, story, or report.
5. Create cartoons using body parts as characters.

   THE DAY THE TEETH MET FLUORIDE
   HEART AND LUNGS DISCUSS
      EXERCISE
   THE RED AND THE WHITE
      OF IT (BLOOD CELLS)

HEALTHY HAVEN EATERY
VEGETARIAN AND NON-VEGE

DRAW OR CUT OUT PIC-
TURES OF FOOD. ATTACH
THEM TO THE VITAMINS.

A D
B1 C
B2 NIACIN

FILMSTRIPS

RUNNING TIPS FOR HEALTH VITAMINS COOKBOOK EXERCISES HEALTH

EXPERIMENT LAB

PROVE OR DISPROVE
PROVE
OR
DISPROVE CARDS TAPE RECORDERS

LEARNING POSSIBILITIES

Understanding the body's nutritional needs
Collecting and recording experimental data
Learning about one's own body

GAMES AND ACTIVITIES

1. Set up an Experiment Lab stocked with statement cards and simple equipment such as microscopes, magnifying glasses, thermometers, stethoscopes, egg timers, and stop watches. Children collect experimental data or written information to prove or disprove the statement on a selected card.

Discussion of the scientific method of collecting data may precede using the Experiment Lab or may grow out of the activity as children compare their findings.

2. Make a game board in the shape of a track on heavy tagboard or cardboard. Write on it tasks and skills that are relevant to your class. Supply a die and markers. This game can be used in the classroom or on the playground.

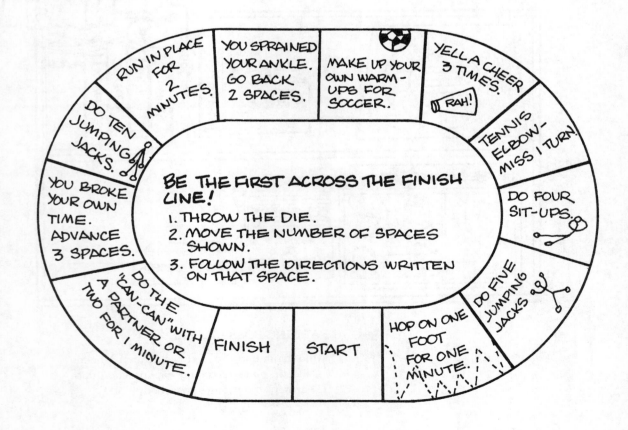

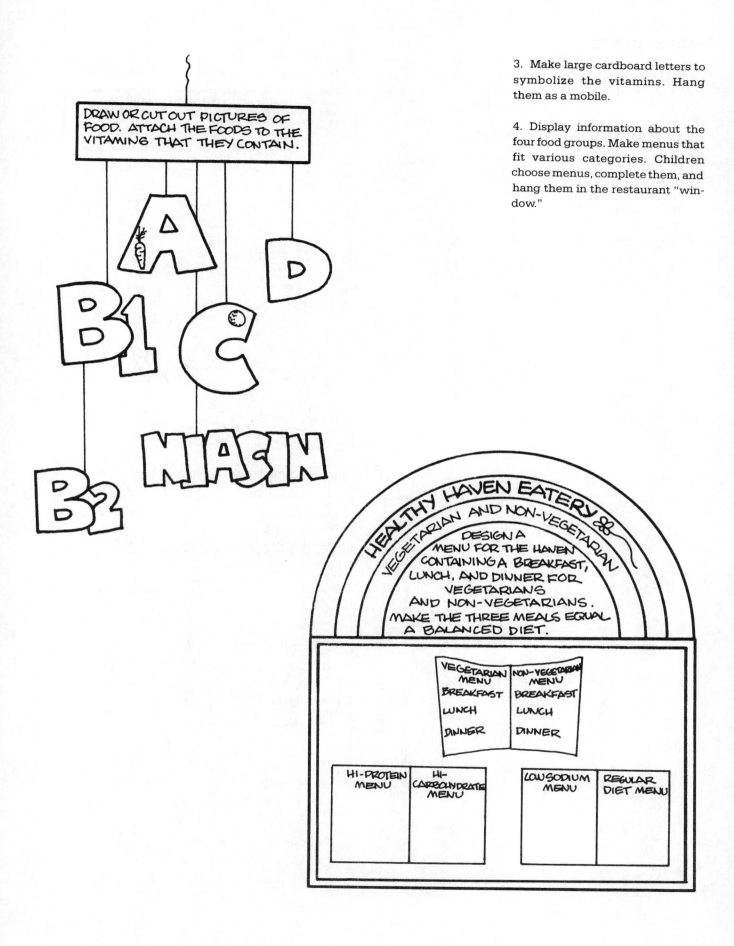

DRAW OR CUT OUT PICTURES OF FOOD. ATTACH THE FOODS TO THE VITAMINS THAT THEY CONTAIN.

A

B1

C

D

NIASIN

B2

3. Make large cardboard letters to symbolize the vitamins. Hang them as a mobile.

4. Display information about the four food groups. Make menus that fit various categories. Children choose menus, complete them, and hang them in the restaurant "window."

HEALTHY HAVEN EATERY

VEGETARIAN AND NON-VEGETARIAN

DESIGN A MENU FOR THE HAVEN CONTAINING A BREAKFAST, LUNCH, AND DINNER FOR VEGETARIANS AND NON-VEGETARIANS. MAKE THE THREE MEALS EQUAL A BALANCED DIET.

VEGETARIAN MENU
BREAKFAST
LUNCH
DINNER

NON-VEGETARIAN MENU
BREAKFAST
LUNCH
DINNER

HI-PROTEIN MENU

HI-CARBOHYDRATE MENU

LOW SODIUM MENU

REGULAR DIET MENU

WORKSHEETS

Name_____ Date_____

FEELING FINE AND OTHERWISE

Make the following observations when you are feeling fine:

Heart: about _____beats per minute

Temperature: about _____

Breathing rate: about _____breaths per minute

Skin color: _____

Other characteristics: _____

But how about when you feel:

sad
Heart_____
Temperature_____
Breathing_____
Skin_____
Other_____

excited
Heart_____
Temperature_____
Breathing_____
Skin_____
Other_____

nervous
Heart_____
Temperature_____
Breathing_____
Skin_____
Other_____

angry
Heart_____
Temperature_____
Breathing_____
Skin_____
Other_____

FULL-SIZE WORKSHEET ON PAGE WS-23

Name_____ Date_____

Different sports and physical activities use and strengthen muscles in different parts of the body. First complete the lists below. Then, using these lists, write the type of sport or physical activity on the part of the body that is exercised.

Sports	Other Physical Activities
_____	_____
_____	_____
_____	_____
_____	_____
_____	_____
_____	_____

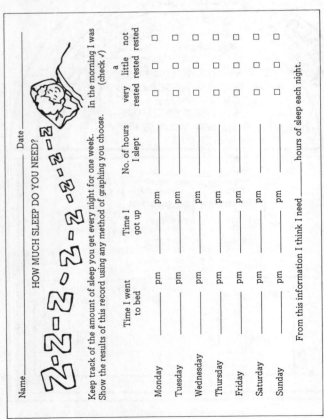

FULL-SIZE WORKSHEET ON PAGE WS-24

Name_____

Date_____

HOW MUCH SLEEP DO YOU NEED?

Keep track of the amount of sleep you get every night for one week. Show the results of this record using any method of graphing you choose.

In the morning I was (check ✓)

very little not rested rested rested

☐ ☐ ☐ ☐ ☐ ☐ ☐
☐ ☐ ☐ ☐ ☐ ☐ ☐
☐ ☐ ☐ ☐ ☐ ☐ ☐

	Time I went to bed	Time I got up	No. of hours I slept
Monday	_____ pm	_____ pm	_____
Tuesday	_____ pm	_____ pm	_____
Wednesday	_____ pm	_____ pm	_____
Thursday	_____ pm	_____ pm	_____
Friday	_____ pm	_____ pm	_____
Saturday	_____ pm	_____ pm	_____
Sunday	_____ pm	_____ pm	_____

From this information I think I need _____ hours of sleep each night.

FULL-SIZE WORKSHEET ON PAGE WS-25

Name _____ Date_____

Fill out this form showing your general body condition and health. Then place it alphabetically in the class file box and check monthly to see if it needs updating.

childhood illnesses:

weight:_____   mumps_____

height_____   measles_____

pulse_____   chicken pox_____

temperature_____   others_____

number of teeth _____

operations _____

allergies _____

number of colds per year _____

description of general health _____

_____

R$_X$ My prescription for better health _____

_____

_____

Literature

The Fairy Tale Castle

EVENTS HAPPENING IN 3's

HAPPY ENDING

"ONCE UPON A TIME"

MAGIC

GOOD & BAD CHARACTERS

Each flag has on it an ingredient of a fairy tale.

Find these ingredients in a fairy tale you have read and put them in the right part of the castle.

F.B.I. FILE

AT THIS CENTER YOU CAN:

1. Write a want ad for a character in a story or book you have read.
2. Interview people at a bookstore to find out how and why they select books. Graph your findings.
3. Write an interview between you, a character from a story or book, and the author of the book.
4. Select a book review from a newspaper or magazine. Read the book. Compare your opinion of the book to the review.
5. Research a Newbery Award recipient. Find out how much of the author's life was included in the book.

GOOD BOOKS

STORY LINE LEGEND

STORY ELEMENTS

LEARNING POSSIBILITIES

Identifying the elements of plot, setting, characterization, mood, and theme that are found in different types of literature

Identifying the components that typify various literary forms: mystery, fairy tale, tall tale

Stimulating interest in reading various forms of literature

Stimulating imaginative writing and thinking

GAMES AND ACTIVITIES

1. Children select several story elements, collect real objects to represent these elements from a story they have read, and attach them to a clothes hanger. A student uses the clothes hanger to lead a "Prop Talk" in which classmates pose questions about the objects on the clothes hanger. "Prop Talks" can also be conducted as a "Twenty Questions" type game. The purpose of the "Prop Talk" is to arouse interest in books.

2. Children make a story line card for a book they have read, using lines from the Story Line Legend Chart or ones they have created. An alternative activity is to make a set of story line cards for the books the class has read. Students are instructed to match titles of books to the correct story line cards.

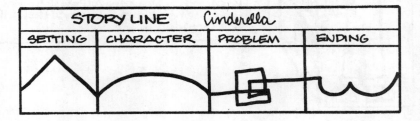

3. Make a set of theme cards for a variety of popular themes found in literature. Children find a theme card to match the theme of the story or book they have read. They write the title and author of the book on a story strip and then weave the story strip through the theme card. Brief statements describing the effects of the theme on plot, style, and mood are written on the story strip where it intersects these elements on the theme card.

4. Make the Fairy Tale Castle chart for the children to use at a bulletin board. After the children have filled the chart with the flags to represent the ingredients of fairy tales, remove the flags from the chart and instruct the children to mix and match them to form the ingredients to write their own fairy tales.

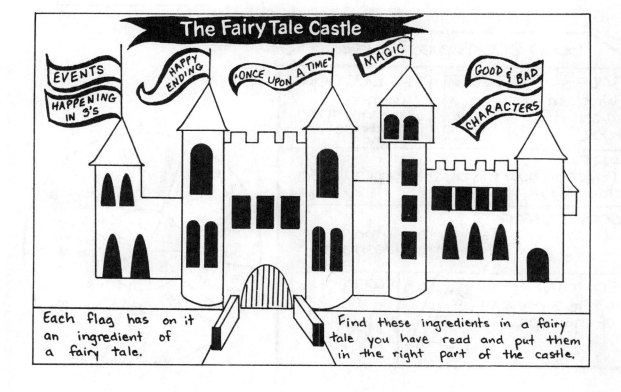

5. Ditto F.B.I. forms onto 5 x 7 cards, and place the cards in a file box. Children complete the cards with information from a mystery story they have read.

6. Children use the spinner to determine the book they will read and the role they will assume in the publishing company. A piece of paper folded into a book can be used to record the work done at the publishing company.

F. B. I. CARD

Book title:_____

Author: _____

Prove it's a mystery. Does it have these elements? Give examples.

EXCITEMENT:_____

CLUES:_____

CRIME:_____

DETECTION:_____

SUSPENSE:_____

Agent Information

Height: _____

Weight:_____

Age:_____

Fingerprint

F.B.I.* FILE

*Famous Book Investigations

GOOD BOOKS PUBLISHING CO.

5 SALES
Write an ad to sell the book.

JAN. SALES

4 PRODUCTION
Gather information about the author.

3 ART
Describe how the art influences the story.

2 COPY EDITOR
Discuss the author's style with a classmate.

1 EDITOR
Write a review of the book.

Rabbit Hill

RECEPTIONIST

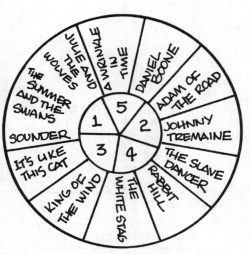

JULIE AND THE WOLVES
A WRINKLE IN TIME
DANIEL BOONE
ADAM OF THE ROAD
THE SUMMER AND THE SWANS
SOUNDER
IT'S LIKE THIS CAT
KING OF THE WIND
THE WHITE STAG
RABBIT HILL
THE SLAVE DANCER
JOHNNY TREMAINE

1 5 2
3 4

7. Children describe each part of a Tall Tale they have read on a 5 x 7 card and then classify the parts into the correct pockets on the chart. After the pockets of the chart have been filled, the cards can be removed from their pockets, shuffled, and reclassified by other students. Used in this way, the activity can also become a matching game.

Paul Bunyan

chopped down 35 trees with one swing of the ax

Paul sneezed and blew down the cook house.

someone had to break up the log jam

WORKSHEETS

Name _____ Date _____

Show which parts of a story are believable and which parts are make believe.

State the reasons for your decisions.

Story Title: _____

Believable		Make Believe	
Part	Reasons	Part	Reasons

FULL-SIZE WORKSHEET ON PAGE WS-26

Name _____ Date _____

Stories often grow out of American history. Research a hero for one of the times on the time line. Use the hero as a character in a mystery, folk tale, or biography.

1725 1750 1775 1800 1825 1850 1875 1900 1925 1950

Hero: _____

Research Findings: _____
_____
_____

Type of Story: _____

Title of Story: _____

Story: _____
_____
_____
_____
_____

FULL-SIZE WORKSHEET ON PAGE WS-27

Name _____ Date _____

CRIME DETECTION LAB

How were the mysteries or crimes solved in the book you have read?

Title of the book _____

Draw or write examples of:

clues _____

detection devices _____

sleuths _____

Now. . .use these mystery parts to write a mystery, fable or fairy tale of your own.

_____
_____
_____
_____
_____
_____
_____

FULL-SIZE WORKSHEET ON PAGE WS-28

Name _____ Date _____

GUESS THE BOOK

1. Use a book you have read with this worksheet.
2. Fill in a different type of clue for the four categories each day.

   Day One — Use a color clue.   Day Four — Use a phrase clue.
   Day Two — Use a symbol clue.   Day Five — Use a sentence clue.
   Day Three — Use a word clue.

3. Display this worksheet for your classmates.
4. Tell your classmates to read the clues to name the book. The first person to name the book you are describing wins the Guess the Book game.

FULL-SIZE WORKSHEET ON PAGE WS-28

Maps

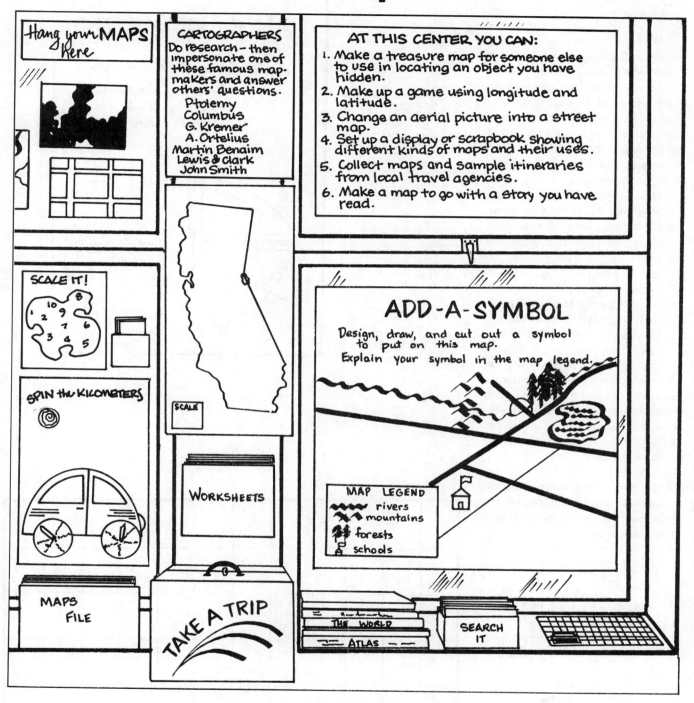

Hang your MAPS here

CARTOGRAPHERS
Do research – then impersonate one of these famous map-makers and answer others' questions.

Ptolemy
Columbus
G. Kremer
A. Ortelius
Martin Benaim
Lewis & Clark
John Smith

AT THIS CENTER YOU CAN:
1. Make a treasure map for someone else to use in locating an object you have hidden.
2. Make up a game using longitude and latitude.
3. Change an aerial picture into a street map.
4. Set up a display or scrapbook showing different kinds of maps and their uses.
5. Collect maps and sample itineraries from local travel agencies.
6. Make a map to go with a story you have read.

SCALE IT!
10 8
1 9
2 7
3 4 5 6

SPIN the KILOMETERS

SCALE

WORKSHEETS

MAPS FILE

TAKE A TRIP

ADD-A-SYMBOL
Design, draw, and cut out a symbol to put on this map.
Explain your symbol in the map legend.

MAP LEGEND
~~~ rivers
^^^ mountains
🌲 forests
⌂ schools

THE WORLD
ATLAS
SEARCH IT

LEARNING POSSIBILITIES

Extending knowledge of geography
Identifying and interpreting various kinds of maps
Using map legends, scales, and latitude and longitude
Making maps
Applying math skills
Learning about famous cartographers

GAMES AND ACTIVITIES

1. Write the names of northern cities on one spinner and southern cities on the other (or use eastern and western cities). Children spin both wheels and measure the distance between the cities shown, using a national or state map hung at the center. Then they record the names of the cities and the distance in kilometers.

This activity could also be used as a game. Each child or team would have its own map and race to compute the distance the fastest.

2. Glue large-squared graph paper onto cardboard to make the game board. Make a set of playing cards, each card stating a direction to move such as "one square north." Provide a paper or toy car for each player. To play, everyone starts in the middle. In turn each child draws a card, follows the directions, and moves his or her car accordingly. The first player to reach any edge of the board wins.

Adapt this game to practicing latitude and longitude skills by labeling lines with degrees, as on a map marked with latitude and longitude lines.

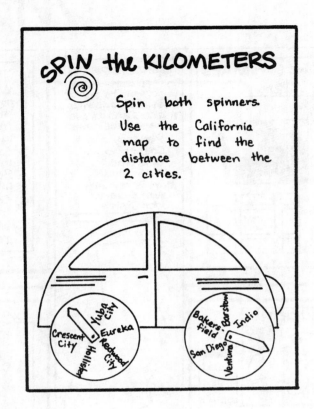

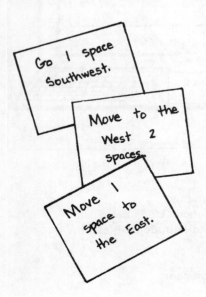

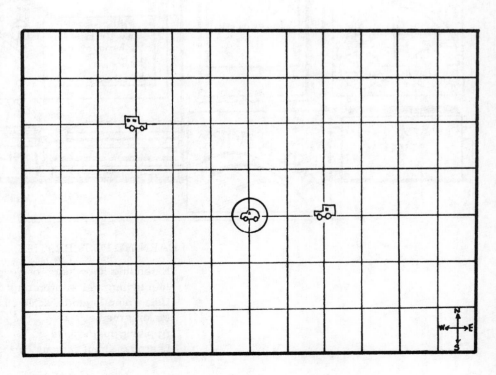

Begin in Omaha. Go on Hwy. 49 South 100 miles. Which cities do you go through?

Which highways would take you most directly from Seattle to Los Angeles?

MY TRAVEL DIARY
Janie W.

3. Make a set of task cards that pose questions based on information found on a given map. Children use the map to find the answers and record them in their travel books. Toy cars may be used to actually "travel" the route.

4. Make a set of cards naming maps that might be included in an atlas. A child picks a card and makes that map to add to the atlas. Multiple copies of outline maps may be provided for children's use.

ATLAS

by John

PRODUCT MAP OF MEXICO

THE ATLAS NEEDS: A MERCATOR PROJECTION MAP

THE ATLAS NEEDS: A POPULATION DENSITY MAP OF OREGON

NEEDS: AN AIRLINE MAP

THE ATLAS NEEDS: A MAP OF MEXICO SHOWING PRODUCTS MADE OR GROWN

THE ATLAS NEEDS: A MAP OF A UNIQUE PLACE SUCH AS THE OCEAN BOTTOM OR OUTER SPACE

5. Scale It!—Make up several strips, writing a different map scale on each one. Draw a simple map of a make-believe place showing 12 numbered locations. Children may enjoy naming the locations.

To play, each player gets a "home location" by rolling the dice one time and writing down the number rolled. Then one player selects a "scale" strip and places it in plain view. Another player rolls the dice 3 additional times. Each player lists these 3 numbers and must then figure out how far each of the 3 locations is from his or her "home" location. Players help each other check their answers.

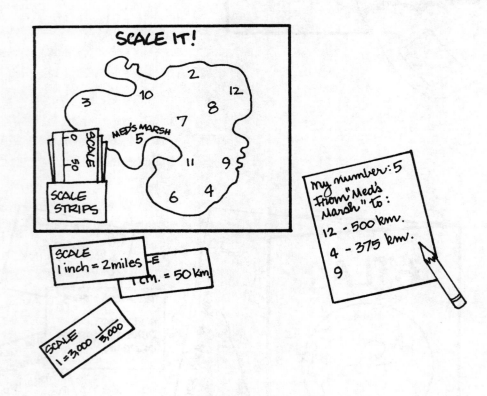

WORKSHEETS

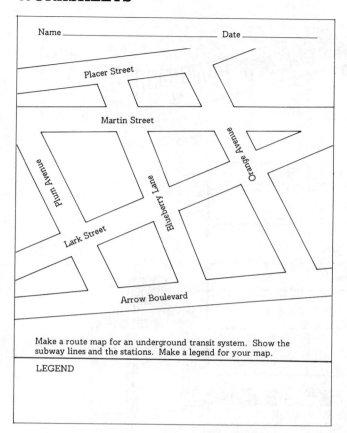

Name_____ Date_____

Placer Street

Martin Street

Plum Avenue

Blueberry Lane

Orange Avenue

Lark Street

Arrow Boulevard

Make a route map for an underground transit system. Show the subway lines and the stations. Make a legend for your map.

LEGEND

Name_____ Date_____

What kind of map would you use to find out . . .

what to wear to visit a new city		
which bus to take		
location of the park		
how people live there		
which mountains are nearby		
which areas have the most people		

FULL-SIZE WORKSHEET ON PAGE WS-29

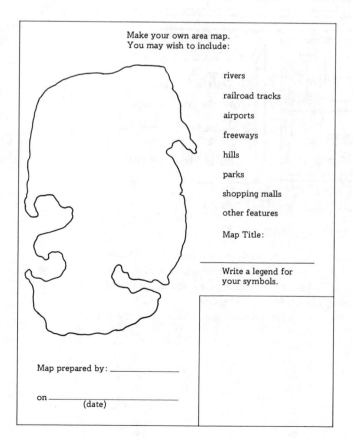

Make your own area map.
You may wish to include:

rivers

railroad tracks

airports

freeways

hills

parks

shopping malls

other features

Map Title:

_____

Write a legend for
your symbols.

Map prepared by : _____

on _____
   (date)

Name_____ Date_____

MAP COLLECTOR CLUB APPLICATION

Name of applicant:_____
Address of applicant:_____
Latitude and longitude of your town:_____
Describe the map you have found to contribute to the club's files:

_____

_____

Tell about your personal interest in maps:_____

_____

Draw a rough outline of your state and show your town's approximate location.

List map activities and skillwork you have completed:
1.
2.
3.
4.

Give this portion of the application to a member of the Map Club, who will then give you 5 questions or tasks related to maps.

Member's name:_____ Applicant's name:_____
Map used:_____
The 5 questions or tasks were: Check if completed satisfactorily:
1. _____
2. _____
3. _____
4. _____
5. _____
Date of test:_____

FULL-SIZE WORKSHEET ON PAGE WS-30

MEASUREMENT

AT THIS CENTER YOU CAN:
1. Drop different things. Use a timer to compare how fast they fall.
2. Collect things that weigh less than a kilogram, between 1 and 2 kilograms, etc.
3. Make a display of different containers that hold the same amount.
4. Measure the length and width of your classroom in meters, centimeters, and milli meters.
5. Create your own unit of measurement. Use it to measure things around you.

Measuring Device used	What it measures
Ruler	
Tape measure	
Stopwatch	

The MAGIC Recipe Box

MEASURING TASKS

Worksheets

What would you use these for?

BUILD IT PATTERNS

Volume Measurers

Linear Measurers

WEIGHING ACTIVITIES

GUESS & PROVE IT BOOKS

GUESS & PROVE IT

BUILD-IT
1. Choose a pattern.
2. Measure to find the pieces you need.
3. Build the doject.

LEARNING POSSIBILITIES

Developing the concept of the standard unit of measure
Learning to use different measuring devices appropriately
Using addition, subtraction, and estimation skills
Learning about fractional parts
Learning to follow written directions and diagrams

NATURAL PIE
10 g. leaves   15 g. twigs
400 ml. water   50 g. sand
Combine all ingredients.
Press into pie plate.

MAKE-BELIEVE MUFFINS
600 g. dirt   90 g. sand
250 ml. water 5 g. grass
Mix ingredients well.
Pour into muffin tins.
Bake in sun until dry.

The -MAGIC- RECIPE BOX

GAMES AND ACTIVITIES

1. Make recipe cards using ingredients found in nature. Put the ingredients at the center or allow children to get them as they need them.

2. Children measure pieces of precut wood and follow the directions on the card to build the object.

3. Place in a box a variety of measuring tools. Children use them to measure objects and then record their data on the chart.

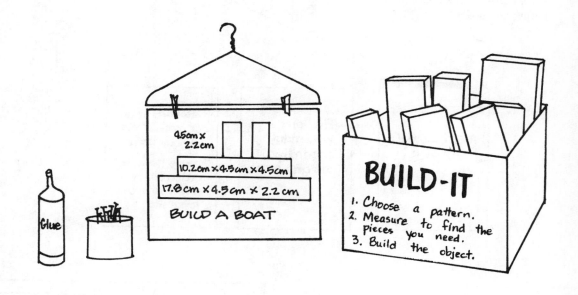

Glue

45 cm x 2.2 cm
10.2 cm x 4.5 cm x 4.5 cm
17.8 cm x 4.5 cm x 2.2 cm

BUILD A BOAT

BUILD-IT
1. Choose a pattern.
2. Measure to find the pieces you need.
3. Build the object.

WHAT WOULD YOU USE THESE FOR?

4. In a box display objects that are different lengths. Children estimate how long an object is and then measure it. They write their estimations and their measurements in their own record books. Provide an answer book.

5. A task card contains one simply stated problem. Children choose a card, do the task, and record their findings in their own record books.

6. In a two-sided folder place a ditto for recording measurements on one side and a form for making a bar graph on the other. The sample worksheet shown is for weight in grams. Additional worksheets may be prepared for other measurements, such as volume in milliliters and liters.

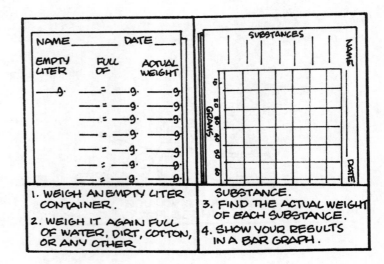

WORKSHEETS

Name_____ Date_____

RAINBOW MEASURING

What will you get when you mix water of various colors together?
Do it and see! Use water with food coloring added to it.

80 ml. red + 40 ml. yellow = _____ ml. _____

20 ml. green + 20 ml. red = _____ ml. _____

10 ml. yellow + 10 ml. red + 10 ml. blue = _____ ml. _____

Now make up your own. Guess what color you think you will get.

Were you right?

My Rainbow Equations:	My guess of color results:	The actual colors I got:
1. _____	_____	_____
2. _____	_____	_____
3. _____	_____	_____

FULL-SIZE WORKSHEET ON PAGE WS-31

Name_____ Date_____

MEASURE AND Enlarge it / Shrink it

Thing measured	As it is	Magnified x 2	Minimized x ½

Name_____ Date_____

COMPARE & COMBINE

Weigh	Most	Least	Make them the same

Weigh	Most	Least	Make them the same

Measure	Longest	Make them the same
	Shortest	

Measure	Longest	Make them the same
	Shortest	

Name_____ Date_____

Gather several containers of different sizes. Estimate how many litres or millilitres each will hold. Use water and a litre measure to check your estimates.

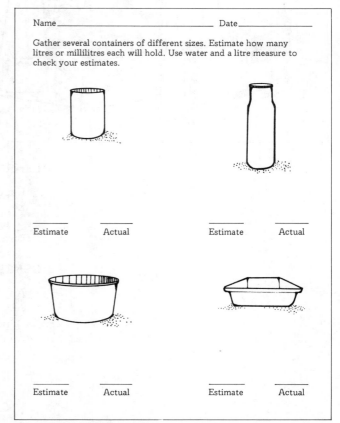

Estimate _____ Actual _____   Estimate _____ Actual _____

Estimate _____ Actual _____   Estimate _____ Actual _____

FULL-SIZE WORKSHEET ON PAGE WS-32

LEARNING POSSIBILITIES

Using simple hand tools

Learning the basic elements common to household appliances and machines

Discovering and exploring how machines work

CENTER NEEDS

An assortment of basic hand tools, such as pliers, adjustable wrench, three screwdrivers (small, medium, large), needle nose pliers, set of nut drivers, and mallet

A minimum collection of broken household appliances with plugs cut off, and, if possible, various shapes of plumbing pipe

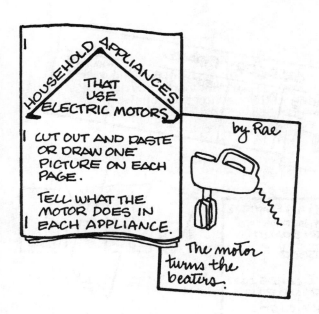

GAMES AND ACTIVITIES

1. Make the large household appliances book out of tagboard. Place in an obvious spot so all children can add to it, read it, and learn from it.

2. Make a Who Am I? chart with blank pockets. Place cards in one and pieces of paper about the same size as the pockets in another.

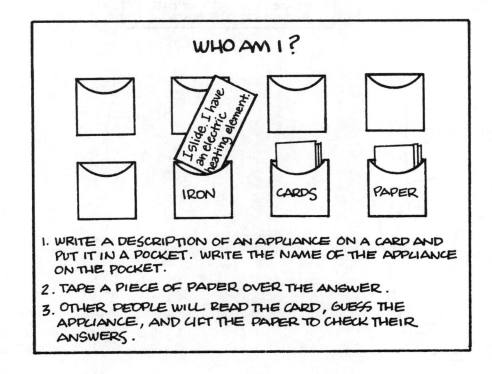

3. Make four large Category Boards, writing the names of the six simple machines across the top. Make a deck of small cards which show objects that are examples of the simple machines on the front and name the matching category of simple machine on the back.

4. Label tagboard with major parts of appliances. Hang on a desk top or full-size chart rack.

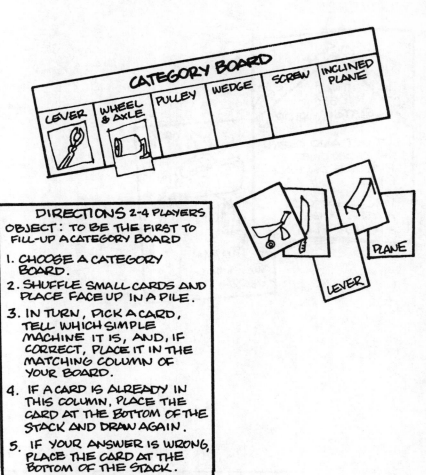

DIRECTIONS 2-4 PLAYERS
OBJECT: TO BE THE FIRST TO FILL-UP A CATEGORY BOARD

1. CHOOSE A CATEGORY BOARD.
2. SHUFFLE SMALL CARDS AND PLACE FACE UP IN A PILE.
3. IN TURN, PICK A CARD, TELL WHICH SIMPLE MACHINE IT IS, AND, IF CORRECT, PLACE IT IN THE MATCHING COLUMN OF YOUR BOARD.
4. IF A CARD IS ALREADY IN THIS COLUMN, PLACE THE CARD AT THE BOTTOM OF THE STACK AND DRAW AGAIN.
5. IF YOUR ANSWER IS WRONG, PLACE THE CARD AT THE BOTTOM OF THE STACK.

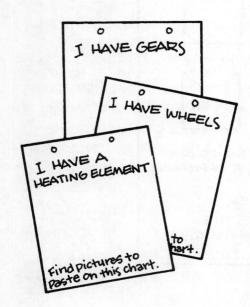

WORKSHEETS

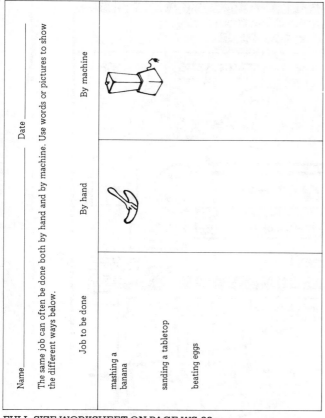

Name _____ Date _____

The same job can often be done both by hand and by machine. Use words or pictures to show the different ways below.

Job to be done	By hand	By machine
mashing a banana		
sanding a tabletop		
beating eggs		

FULL-SIZE WORKSHEET ON PAGE WS-33

Name _____ Date _____

PLUMBING PIPE

1. Use pipe to construct a duplicate of the pipes under the sink and the drinking fountain outside. Draw or name other things you can duplicate with pipe, such as swings, bannisters, etc.

2. Name the shapes of pipe used in the sink or drinking fountain.

3. Design on the back of this paper something "new" which can be built from pipe.

   What pieces do you need?_____

   How many of each type?_____

   How long?_____

   How will the object be used?_____

   BUILD IT!

Name _____ Date _____

FIND MACHINES THAT DO THE SAME KIND OF WORK AS THE TOOL

(For example, a screwdriver turns; what machines turn?)
Cut out or draw pictures to show them.

TOOLS	MACHINES

Name _____ Date _____

MACHINE TAKE-APART

1. Choose an item to take apart.
   Name it._____
   _____

2. Is it electric?_____ If yes, does it have an electric motor?_____
   If yes, tell what the motor does. _____
   _____

3. Does it have an electric heating element? _____
   If yes, where is it and what does it heat?_____
   _____

4. If it's not electric, what makes it work?_____
   _____

5. Draw a diagram of how the item works.

FULL-SIZE WORKSHEET ON PAGE WS-34

Media

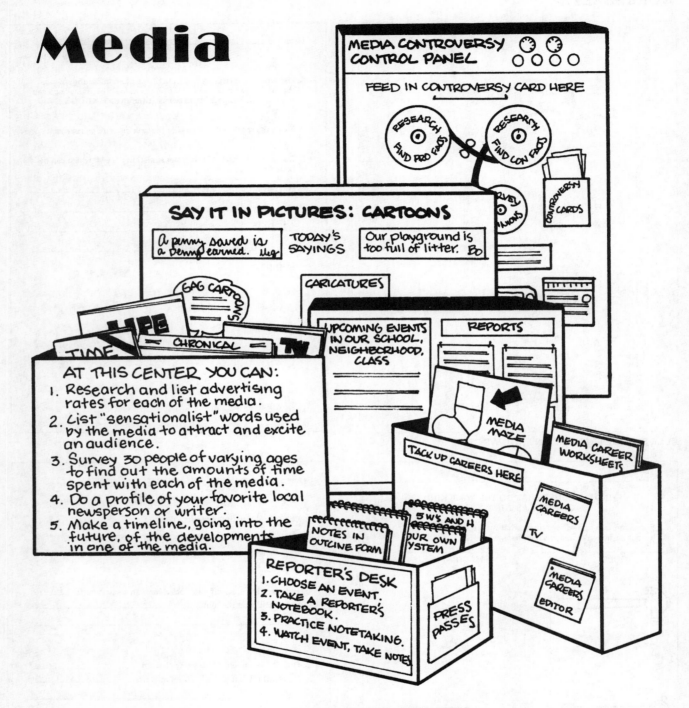

MEDIA CONTROVERSY CONTROL PANEL

FEED IN CONTROVERSY CARD HERE

RESEARCH FIND PRO FACTS

RESEARCH FIND CON FACTS

CONTROVERSY CARDS

SAY IT IN PICTURES: CARTOONS

A penny saved is a penny earned. Meg

TODAY'S SAYINGS

Our playground is too full of litter. Bo

GAG CARTOONS

CARICATURES

TIME LIFE CHRONICAL TV

UPCOMING EVENTS IN OUR SCHOOL, NEIGHBORHOOD, CLASS

REPORTS

MEDIA MAZE

MEDIA CAREER WORKSHEETS

TACK UP CAREERS HERE

MEDIA CAREERS TV

AT THIS CENTER YOU CAN:
1. Research and list advertising rates for each of the media.
2. List "sensationalist" words used by the media to attract and excite an audience.
3. Survey 30 people of varying ages to find out the amounts of time spent with each of the media.
4. Do a profile of your favorite local newsperson or writer.
5. Make a timeline, going into the future, of the developments in one of the media.

NOTES IN OUTLINE FORM

5 W'S AND H OUR OWN SYSTEM

REPORTER'S DESK
1. CHOOSE AN EVENT.
2. TAKE A REPORTER'S NOTEBOOK.
3. PRACTICE NOTETAKING.
4. WATCH EVENT, TAKE NOTES.

PRESS PASSES

MEDIA CAREERS EDITOR

LEARNING POSSIBILITIES

Combining facts and opinions to create a product
Developing note-taking skills
Learning and practicing cartooning methods
Developing observation skills
Making inferences and judgments
Comparing and contrasting written and broadcast information
Career education

GAMES AND ACTIVITIES

1. Make a Control Panel and a set of controversy cards. Buttons and beads make good knobs, and ribbon spools can be the reels. Children choose a controversy card, accumulate pro and con facts by doing research, and gather pro and con opinions by surveying classmates and other people.

Controversy Card suggestions:

Newspapers cover too much sensational news (violence, hardship, etc.).

The "ratings" are not a realistic view of what makes good television and radio.

Radio plays too much music—it needs more plays, interviews, and informational programming.

One night a month, each TV station should poll viewers to see what they are watching. It should be different viewers each month.

Newspapers carry the same basic story, day after day, with very little change.

Newscasters are picked for looks and personality, not for reporting ability.

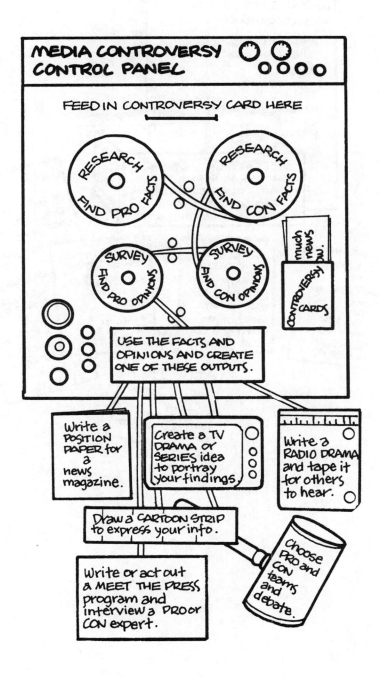

2. Post an "Upcoming Events" chart and have children help you keep it current. Make Reporter's Notebooks out of steno pads. On the cover of each pad write examples of a different method of note taking. A child selects an event from the chart and a Reporter's Notebook, then "covers" the event, takes notes, and later transcribes the notes and prepares a report. Reports may be taped (as for radio), videotaped, or written (as for a newspaper or magazine).

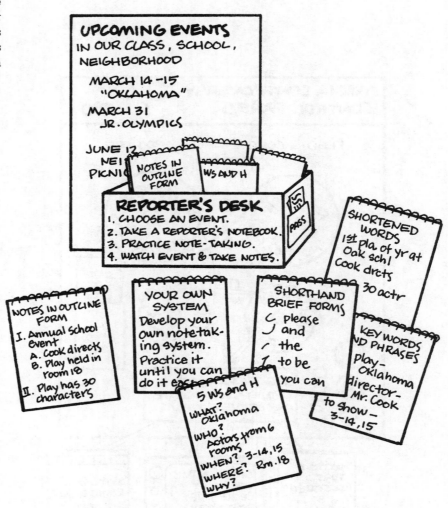

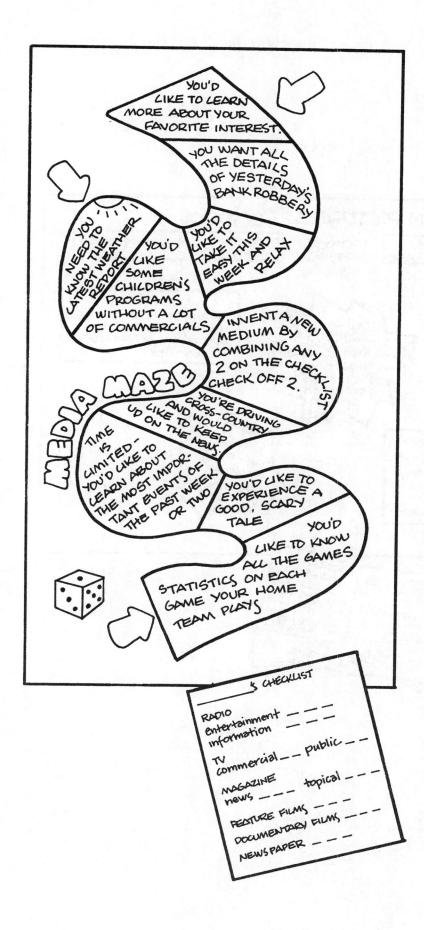

3. Make a Media Maze gameboard and multiple copies of a checklist that reflects the media being studied. Players may enter and reenter the gameboard at any arrow. To play, each player, in turn, rolls the die, moves the indicated number of steps, and reads the situation landed on. The player then decides which of the media would best fill the need described in the situation. When the selection of media has been explained satisfactorily to the group, the player may check it on the checklist. The first player to fill the whole checklist is the winner.

4. Set up Say It in Pictures as a chart or bulletin board. Children can help collect samples of each type of cartoon for a samples booklet and can contribute to the homilies and problems to be cartooned each day.

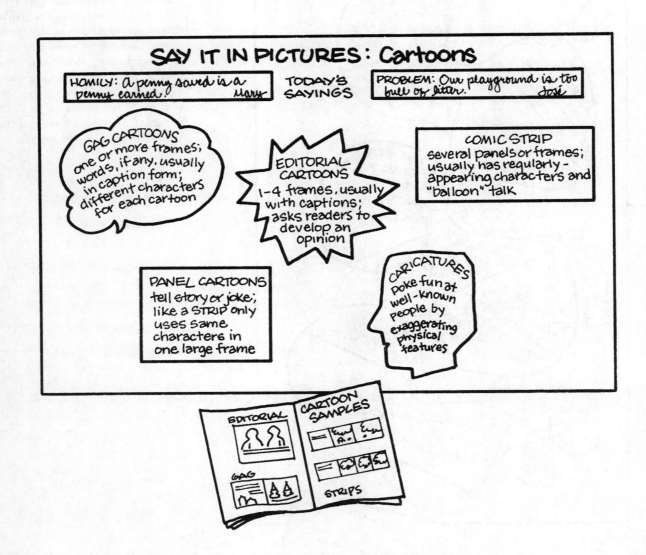

WORKSHEETS

1

Career Title _____

Illustration
(draw or cut out
and paste)

Check any media in which one might find employment:
- ☐ newspapers
- ☐ news magazines
- ☐ topical magazines
  name type: _____
- ☐ documentary film
- ☐ recording industry
- ☐ TV-entertainment
- ☐ TV-news, public affairs
- ☐ radio-entertainment
- ☐ feature films

List any related fields in which employment may be found:
_____

MEDIA CAREER GUIDE _____
(career title)

4

RESOURCE LIST to help you learn more about the job

Books: _____

Films, TV shows, etc. _____

Companies/People to visit or interview: _____

Author of article: _____

MEDIA CAREER GUIDE

FULL-SIZE WORKSHEET ON PAGE WS-35

3

EDUCATION _____

OTHER TRAINING _____

MEDIA CAREER GUIDE

2

JOB HIGHLIGHTS – a brief description of activities, pay range, benefits, etc.
_____

JOB QUALIFICATIONS – personal qualities, talents, and interests other than education
_____

MEDIA CAREER GUIDE

FULL-SIZE WORKSHEET ON PAGE WS-36

Name _____ Date _____

MEDIA PRODUCTION FLOW CHART

1. Choose one of the media to learn about and do research.

2. In words and pictures fill in the flow chart to show the main steps of the production process.

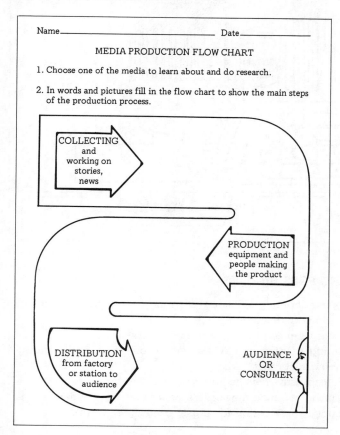

COLLECTING and working on stories, news

PRODUCTION equipment and people making the product

DISTRIBUTION from factory or station to audience

AUDIENCE OR CONSUMER

Name _____ Date _____

MEDIA NEWS COVERAGE

1. Choose one story from the TV evening news. Briefly describe it in the DAY 1 box below.

2. Find the same story in the newspaper and on the radio news and note changes, additions, or nonappearances.

3. Follow the story in all three media for two more days noting any likenesses and differences in the way the story is covered.

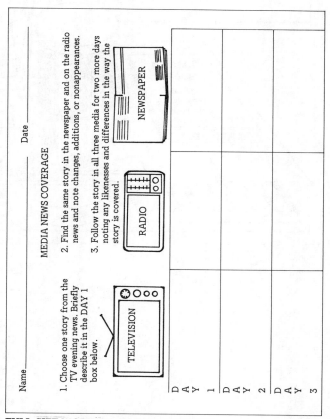

TELEVISION   RADIO   NEWSPAPER

DAY 1
DAY 2
DAY 3

FULL-SIZE WORKSHEET ON PAGE WS-37

MUSIC ♫

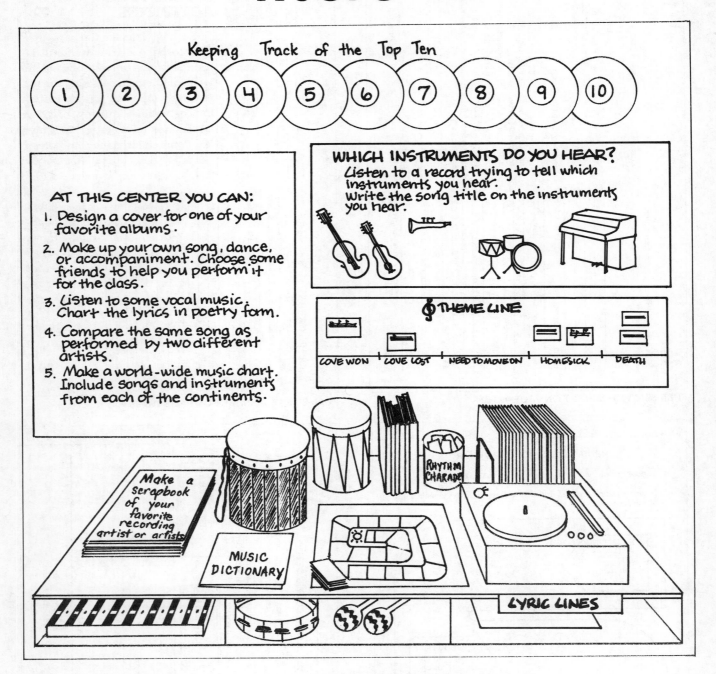

Keeping Track of the Top Ten

① ② ③ ④ ⑤ ⑥ ⑦ ⑧ ⑨ ⑩

AT THIS CENTER YOU CAN:

1. Design a cover for one of your favorite albums.
2. Make up your own song, dance, or accompaniment. Choose some friends to help you perform it for the class.
3. Listen to some vocal music. Chart the lyrics in poetry form.
4. Compare the same song as performed by two different artists.
5. Make a world-wide music chart. Include songs and instruments from each of the continents.

WHICH INSTRUMENTS DO YOU HEAR?
Listen to a record trying to tell which instruments you hear.
Write the song title on the instruments you hear.

THEME LINE

LOVE WON | LOVE LOST | NEED TO MOVE ON | HOMESICK | DEATH

Make a scrapbook of your favorite recording artist or artists

MUSIC DICTIONARY

RHYTHM CHARADE

LYRIC LINES

LEARNING POSSIBILITIES

Developing listening skills and learning to recognize the sounds of various instruments

Translating music into its rhythmic components

Stimulating reading and writing about current popular music

Developing dictionary skills

Learning to draw conclusions from survey data

Recognizing common musical elements in various types of music

Developing appreciation for music from other countries

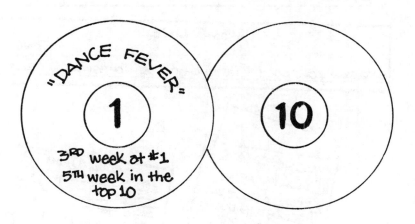

GAMES AND ACTIVITIES

1. Each week make ten paper records to hang at the center. Children write the top ten songs of the week on them. In selecting the top ten, they may use a radio station list or take a survey of their classmates to make up their own list. Some children may enjoy keeping tallies of records that are in the top ten for several weeks.

2. Place large construction paper and yarn of various colors at the center for children to use in making scrapbooks. In these scrapbooks children may keep pictures, newsclips, and information about their favorite recording artist or artists.

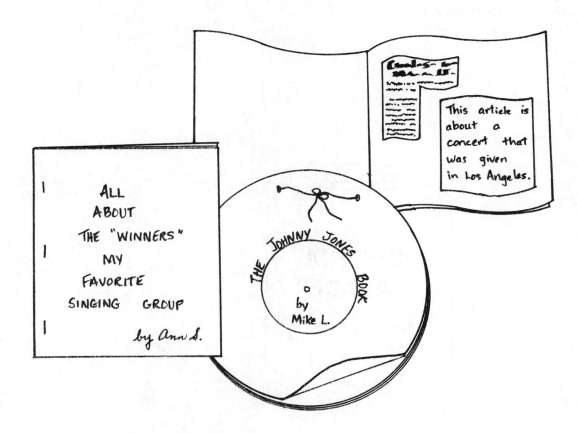

3. Start two Lyric Lines: one, a time line naming general eras of American history and a second line naming some common themes. Make available books and records that contain American folk songs. Draw a set of song cards, each one showing a measure containing from one to six notes but no words. Children draw a song card from the envelope, and using the books and records as references, retell an American folk song using the same number of sentences as there are notes on the song card. Finished cards are then placed in an appropriate place on one of the Lyric Lines.

4. Make a set of cards with a current song title written on each. The children form two teams. One player draws a card and must clap out the rhythm of part of the song to his teammates. If his team guesses correctly within one minute, it earns one point. Teams take turns acting out rhythms until all the cards are used or time is up.

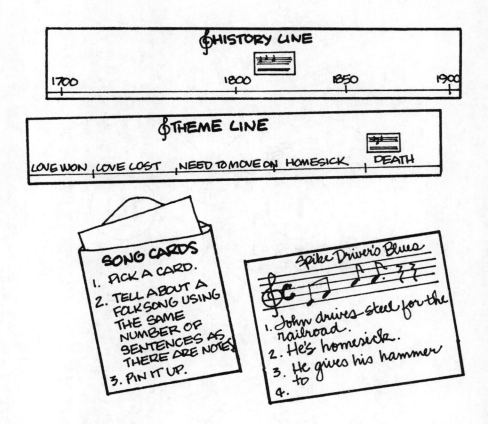

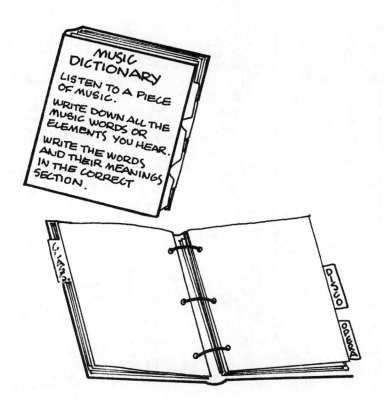

5. Set up a looseleaf or composition booklet as a dictionary. Divide the book into sections, naming types of music your class is studying, such as disco, jazz, classical, rock, and opera. Within each section make a set of A to Z pages. Children add words, definitions, respellings if needed, and perhaps drawings to the dictionary. Groups of children may be assigned responsibility for the various sections.

6. Make a set of cards with questions about current recordings, artists, instruments, etc. Write the number of spaces to advance if the answer is correct. Put the answers on the backs of the cards and write "chance-type" directions on the game board, which will make the game more exciting.

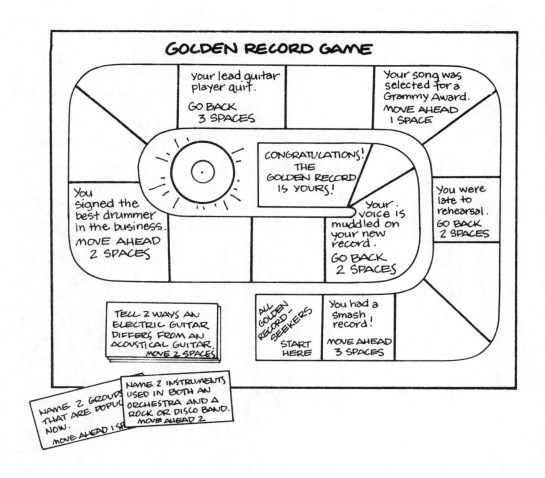

WORKSHEETS

Name_____ Date_____

Take a survey of people's favorite songs.
What conclusions can you make based on your survey?

Favorite Song	Age of Person Surveyed	Occupation	Average time spent listening to radio per day

Conclusions:

Make up another music survey.

Name_____ Date_____

FOR DEE JAYS ONLY

Plan an hour's listening time for a radio audience. Describe the audience you are planning for:_____

Record Title	Recording Artist	Playing Time (must add up to 60 minutes)
		Total Time = 60 min.

Name_____

Date_____

MUSIC: NOW and THEN

Choose 3 classical pieces to listen to and write their names below.

List the names of 3 popular songs you know.

Write similarities between the classical and popular pieces. Use the words at the bottom of the page or other words you know.

1._____
2._____
3._____

INSTRUMENTS: percussion strings horns electronic drums piano solo duet

MELODY: smooth sweet-sounding rising and falling

TEMPO: fast slow break-neck

RHYTHM: catchy even smooth hard

FULL-SIZE WORKSHEET ON PAGE WS-38

_____'S LISTENING RECORD

1. Listen to two selections from each category named on the grooves. On the same groove, write in titles, composers, performers (if possible).

2. Mark each selection with one of these ratings:

   + would like to hear again soon

   o would be OK to hear again someday

   - wouldn't like to hear again

   * would like to hear other things from this category

ETHNIC OR FROM ANOTHER COUNTRY
THE 3 BS - BACH, BEETHOVEN, BRAHMS
ROCK OR OTHER CONTEMPORARY MUSIC
DATES I LISTENED
OPERA (ARIAS)
INSTRUMENTAL SOLO
THE BLUES OR COUNTRY

FULL-SIZE WORKSHEET ON PAGE WS-39

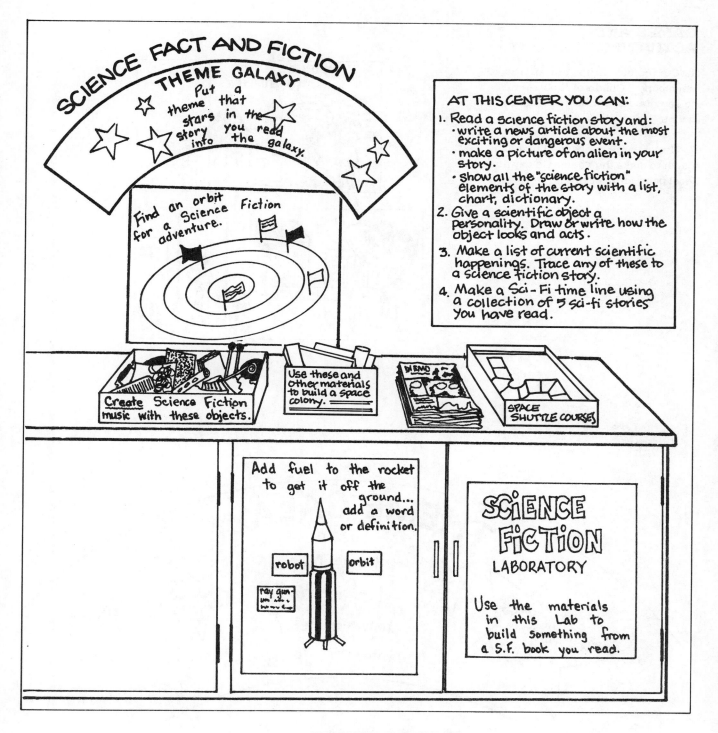

LEARNING POSSIBILITIES

Stimulating reading and creative writing

Recognizing the theme of a story and being able to write from a given theme

Transforming real-life situations into imaginary ones

Categorizing

Matching auditory images to verbal or visual images by creating music

GAMES AND ACTIVITIES

1. Cut comic strips out of the newspaper. Children choose one to rewrite and redraw as science fiction.

2. Use a large piece of butcher paper to make the Theme Galaxy a focal point for the center.

3. On flags, children write adventures from their stories and place them in the right orbits.

4. Children use the materials to create their own science fiction music to accompany stories they have read or written.

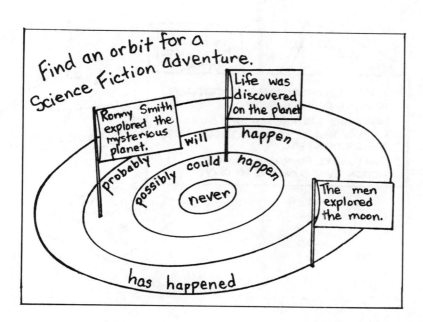

Find an orbit for a Science Fiction adventure.

Rormy Smith explored the mysterious planet.

Life was discovered on the planet

probably   will   happen

possibly   could   happen

never

The men explored the moon.

has happened

PLANETARY VIBRATIONS
Music for 2 voices and instruments
by Steven P.

1st voice

Create Science Fiction music with these objects.

5. Place materials for building a space colony in a box. Hang finished work from the ceiling.

6. Make Space Shuttle Courses with blank spaces. Cut pieces of heavy paper to fit on the spaces. Place papers in an envelope next to the courses.

USE THESE AND OTHER MATERIALS TO BUILD A SPACE COLONY.

DESCRIBE THE PEOPLE WHO LIVE THERE, THEIR "HOMES", THEIR FOOD, THEIR WORK, ETC.

THEN WRITE YOUR OWN SCIENCE FICTION BASED ON THE COLONY.

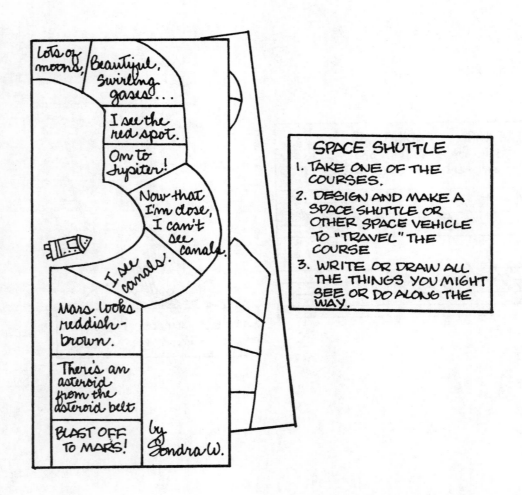

SPACE SHUTTLE

1. TAKE ONE OF THE COURSES.
2. DESIGN AND MAKE A SPACE SHUTTLE OR OTHER SPACE VEHICLE TO "TRAVEL" THE COURSE
3. WRITE OR DRAW ALL THE THINGS YOU MIGHT SEE OR DO ALONG THE WAY.

WORKSHEETS

Name_____ Date_____

Read a science fiction story. List elements from your story in the correct category.

Fun	Harmful	Helpful	Frightening

Name_____ Date_____

MATCH **SCIENCE FICTION TO SCIENCE NONFICTION**

Find things in Science Fiction stories which can be put into these real scientific categories.

Space Vehicles	Natural Phenomena
Tools & Equipment	Uniforms

FULL-SIZE WORKSHEET ON PAGE WS-40

Name_____ Date_____

Create the course that finishes the story by writing a part of it on each rocket.

Problem: Two space vehicles from different countries are on a "crash" course in space.

Solution: The Interplanetary Traffic Control Agency felt satisfied with their decision.

Name_____ Date_____

DO YOU WANT TO BE AN ASTRONAUT?

Find out what it takes to be an astronaut.

Age_____ Sex_____

Education_____

Physical requirements_____

Other requirements_____

Scientific Knowledge Needed_____

What training does a person go through to become an astronaut?

_____

If you are turned down as an astronaut, what other space-related jobs might be exciting? List 6.

1._____   4._____

2._____   5._____

3._____   6._____

FULL-SIZE WORKSHEET ON PAGE WS-41

SEQUENCE

AT THIS CENTER YOU CAN:

1. Draw pictures of things that are kept in order.
2. Make a collection of step-by-step instructions. Order them from simple to hard to understand.
3. Give a friend written and verbal directions to make something. Ask your friend which directions were easier to follow and why.
4. Cut up a set of directions. Give them to a friend to put in order.
5. Retell a story from your favorite television show

WORKSHEETS

THINGS to ORDER
• HOLIDAYS
• TV SHOWS
• FILMS
• RECORDS
• PEOPLE IN SCHOOL

THINGS TO MAKE
• kite
• beanbag
• bird cage
• doll house

COMMAND

LEARNING POSSIBILITIES

Sequencing words, story parts, events and directions
Identifying the logical sequence in which things are done
Recognizing that time changes things

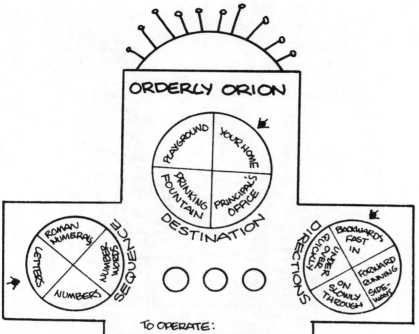

ORDERLY ORION

DESTINATION

PLAYGROUND
YOUR HOME
DRINKING FOUNTAIN
PRINCIPAL'S OFFICE

SEQUENCE

ROMAN NUMERALS
LETTERS
NUMBER WORDS
NUMBERS

DIRECTIONS

BACKWARDS
FAST
IN
UNDER
OVER
QUICKLY
ON
SLOWLY
THROUGH
FORWARD
RUNNING
SIDEWAYS

GAMES AND ACTIVITIES

1. Make a robot out of cardboard, and attach four spinners labeled Destination, Sequence, Directions, and Command. After spinning each of the dials, children describe the sequence of commands needed to get the robot to the destination. Provide a simple worksheet for children to record their responses (see page 125.)

TO OPERATE:

1. Spin DESTINATION dial to find out where Orion will go.

2. Spin SEQUENCE dial to find out how to list the steps that will get Orion to his destination.

3. Spin DIRECTIONS dial to find the words to be used in Orion's commands. Each word must be used in a separate sentence.

4. Use the worksheet to record your work.

COMMAND ORDERLY ORION

COMMANDER _____   DATE _____

DESTINATION	DIRECTIONS Words to be used in Orion's commands	SEQUENCE	ORION'S COMMANDS
Principal's office	under	first	Walk under the green arch.
	over	second	Go over the overpass and to the door marked Office.
	quickly	third	Move quickly to the door labeled Mrs. Content.

2. Children choose something to order from the Things to Order list. They select a rating continuum to order it. After tracing around the selected rating continuum on a blank sheet of paper, they label their continuum to match the one that was traced and use it as a worksheet for their responses.

3. Children roll a die and move the number of spaces indicated on the die. Players who move into the circle must use the number on the space where they have landed as the number of steps they will describe to get out of the situation named in the circle.

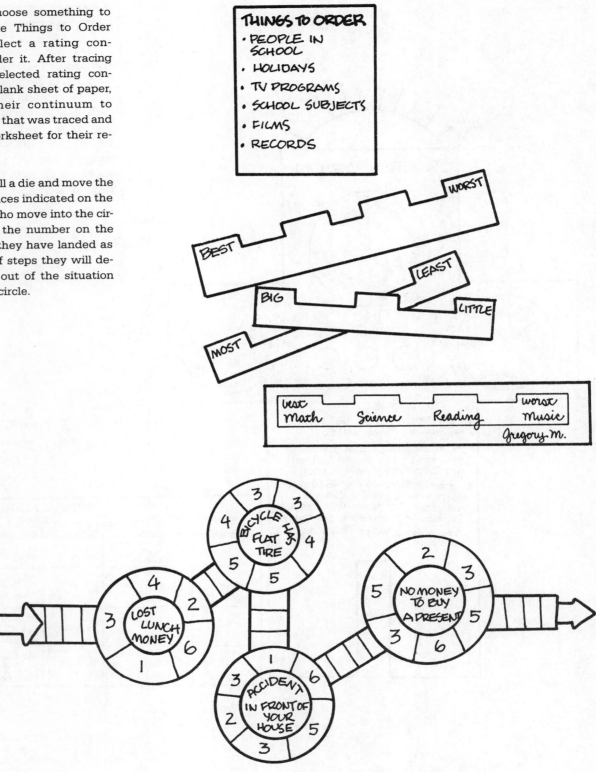

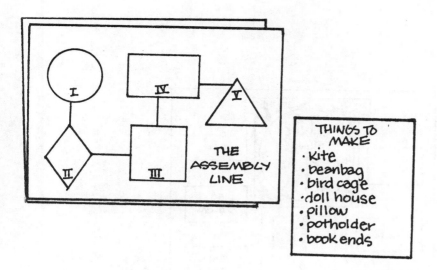

THINGS TO MAKE
- kite
- beanbag
- bird cage
- doll house
- pillow
- potholder
- book ends

THE ASSEMBLY LINE

4. Cover the Assembly Line flow charts with clear contact. Use numbers, Roman numerals, the alphabet, etc., to indicate the sequence for the flow chart. Children select an object to make from a list provided for them, make the object, and use the Assembly Line flow chart to show the order in which the object was made.

5. Write the parts of a story on 3 x 5 cards or cut out a story from an old book and paste it onto cards. Number the cards on the back to show the correct sequence. For primary students, color code the cards for each story to aid in sorting.

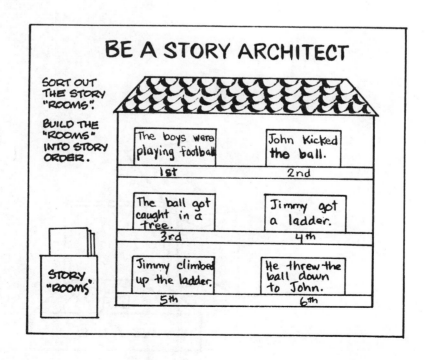

6. Children select an object from the chart. Provide children with a simple clock pattern to trace around. They then use the clock outline to record their response of how the selected object changed over time.

7. Collect tools and materials related to real-life tasks and store them in boxes. On one side of the box describe the task. On the lid give the number of steps needed to do the task. Leave space on the lid for children to sequentially place the tools and materials they used to perform the task.

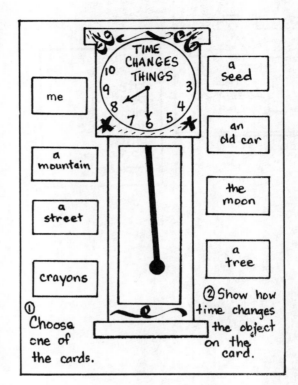

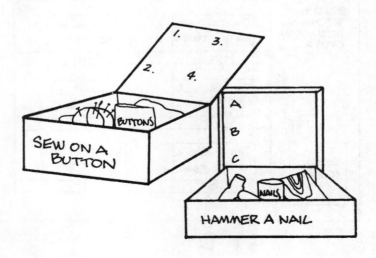

WORKSHEETS

Name _____ Date _____

CAREERS LIMITED APPLICATION FORM

Imagine that you are applying for one of these careers:

- firefighter
- interior decorator
- used car dealer
- gardener
- astronaut
- dance instructor
- nurse
- secretary
- garbage collector

Select a career and complete the application form.

1. Career choice _____

2. Background experiences qualifying you for the career

_____

3. Knowledge of the career

_____

   List types of jobs related to the career.

_____

_____

_____

4. Career performance

   Select a job related to the career and describe the steps you would take to do it.   Job _____

First _____
Second _____
Third _____
Fourth _____
Fifth _____

FULL-SIZE WORKSHEET ON PAGE WS-42

Name _____ Date _____

WHAT DID YOU DO?

Keep a log of what you do during two days. How and why do the days compare?

Time	One Day	Another Day	How the Days Are Alike and Different	Why the Days Are Alike and Different
8:30 A.M.				
9:00 A.M.				
10:30 A.M.				
12:00 P.M.				
2:25 P.M.				
4:15 P.M.				
6:30 P.M.				
8:45 P.M.				

Name _____ Date _____

STITCH-A-SENTENCE

1. Number the words in order for each sentence.
2. Use a needle and thread to sew the words together to make a sentence.

The		bought
girl	a	
		toy

slipped	silently	the
seal		
the	into	
harbor.		

	for	
	before	cars
always		
	street	
watch		
	you	
cross		
	the	

the	to	
time	stitch	
is	take	Now	a

FULL-SIZE WORKSHEET ON PAGE WS-43

COMMAND ORDERLY ORION

Commander _____ Date _____

Destination	Commands Used to Get to the Destination	Order	Actions Taken to Get to the Destination
		First	
		Second	
		Third	

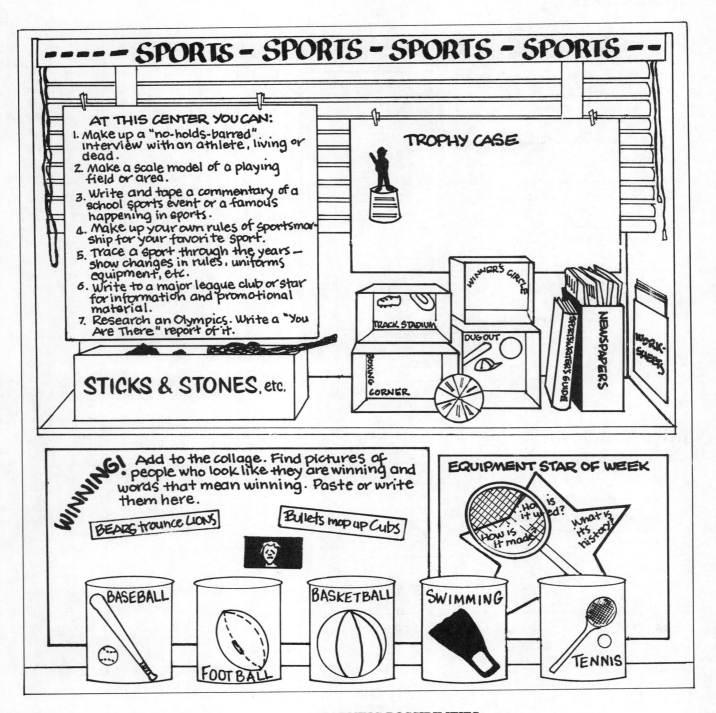

LEARNING POSSIBILITIES

Comparing past and present through the study of sports, Olympics, etc.

Developing the vocabulary and techniques of news reporting and page layout

Categorizing

Making inferences about people's feelings from their bodily and facial expressions

Using creative thinking to develop original games

Making judgments related to developments in sports

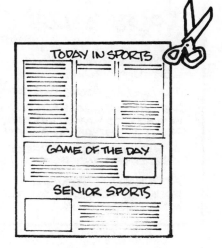

GAMES AND ACTIVITIES

1. Children "tryout" as a sports page editor by cutting up articles from one day's sports page or section of the newspaper and reassembling them into new categories. Some of these categories might be columns, sections, or special interest articles titled: "Sports for Health," "Sports World News," "Game of the Day," "Off-Season Sports News," "Notable Numbers in Sports," "Senior Sports News," and "And the Bid Goes On—Money in Sports." Your local paper's sports editor or writers may be available to discuss layout techniques and sports coverage ideas.

2. In a box place some objects that could be used in a game, such as sticks, a stone, cans, ropes, balls, some chalk, etc.

3. Label ice cream containers with the names of sports. Children write sports words on cards and drop the cards in the correct cartons.

   To play as a game, one child stands behind each sports can. The player who is "it" throws a beanbag in one of the containers. The person standing behind it must name a word that goes with that sport. If she can, "it" must throw again. If she can't, she becomes the new "it." The object is to keep from becoming "it."

STICKS & STONES, etc.

Choose 2 things from the box and make up your own game. Remember to include the playing area, the number of players, the rules, and the object of the game.

4. Have the children bring their baseball or other sports trading cards to school for this game.

5. Set up a class "Sportswriter's Guide: Special Sports Vocabulary" or have individual children or small groups make their own. Include a section for each sport containing several pages. Children list, alphabetically, terminology particular to the sports and give definitions. Illustrations, diagrams, and respellings may be included, where appropriate. Be sure to include any unusual sports or activities that may be unique to your school or town, as well as ones invented by children, such as from the "Sticks and Stones" activity on page 127.

6. Design a large sheet of butcher paper or a series of shallow boxes to represent the Hall of Records. Name the various rooms. Provide a spinner labeled with names of a wide variety of sports and athletic events.

Children spin the spinner and research the sport they land on. They write a record or famous first on a cut-out of an appropriate object and place it in the sports "room." The objects can later be regrouped into new categories, such as "Firsts," "Long Distance Records," "Women's Records," "Most-Times Records."

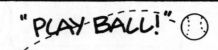

"PLAY BALL!"

PLAYERS STAND IN A LINE OR SIT IN A CIRCLE.

THE CALLER HOLDS THE CARDS.

THE CALLER ASKS EACH PLAYER, IN TURN, TO NAME ONE FACT ABOUT A PERSON ON A CARD.

IF THE ANSWER IS CORRECT, THE PLAYER KEEPS THE CARD.

AT THE END OF SEVERAL ROUNDS, PLAYER WITH THE MOST CARDS WINS.

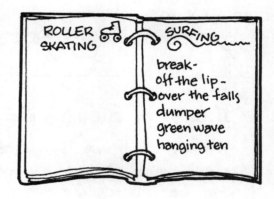

ROLLER SKATING

SURFING

break-
off the lip-
over the falls
dumper
green wave
hanging ten

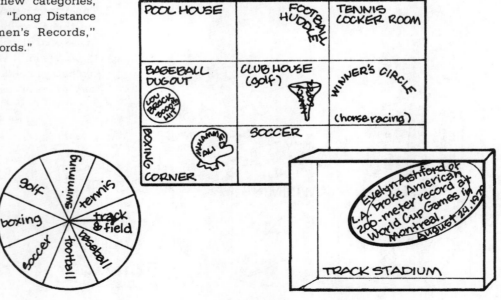

POOL HOUSE · FOOTBALL HUDDLE · TENNIS LOCKER ROOM · BASEBALL DUGOUT · CLUB HOUSE (golf) · WINNER'S CIRCLE (horse racing) · BOXING CORNER · SOCCER

Evelyn Ashford of L.A. broke American 200-meter record at World Cup Games in Montreal, August 24, 1979

TRACK STADIUM

golf · swimming · tennis · boxing · track & field · soccer · football · baseball

WORKSHEETS

SPORTS: THE UPS AND THE DOWNS

SPORT:_____

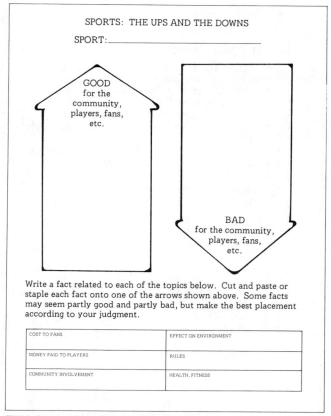

GOOD for the community, players, fans, etc.

BAD for the community, players, fans, etc.

Write a fact related to each of the topics below. Cut and paste or staple each fact onto one of the arrows shown above. Some facts may seem partly good and partly bad, but make the best placement according to your judgment.

COST TO FANS	EFFECT ON ENVIRONMENT
MONEY PAID TO PLAYERS	RULES
COMMUNITY INVOLVEMENT	HEALTH, FITNESS

FULL-SIZE WORKSHEET ON PAGE WS-44

WHAT DO YOU KNOW ABOUT THESE SPORTS?

Name _____ Date _____

Sport	Country of Origin	Equipment	Number of Players	Playing Area
Bicycle racing				
Billiards				
Birling				
Croquet				
Curling				
Epee fencing				
Jai alai				
Lacrosse				
Lawn bowling				
Polo				
Quoits				
Rowing				
Rugby				
Shuffleboard				
Skeet				
Squash				

FULL-SIZE WORKSHEET ON PAGE WS-45

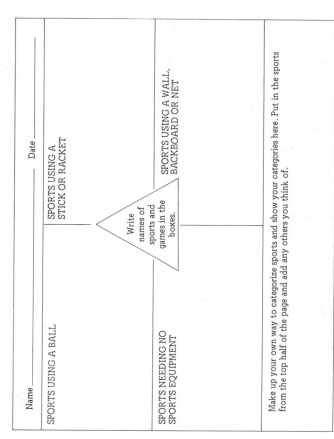

Name _____ Date _____

SPORTS USING A STICK OR RACKET

SPORTS USING A WALL, BACKBOARD OR NET

Write names of sports and games in the boxes.

SPORTS USING A BALL

SPORTS NEEDING NO SPORTS EQUIPMENT

Make up your own way to categorize sports and show your categories here. Put in the sports from the top half of the page and add any others you think of.

Name _____ Date _____

SPORTS CRAZES AND FADS

1900-1920   20s

Choose one of these sports and design a contest or competition for it. Fill in the vital facts below.

30s   40s

_____ CONTEST

WHAT HAPPENS: _____

50s   60s

RULES: _____

WHERE IT WILL BE HELD: _____

70s

QUALIFICATIONS AND LIMITATION FOR ENTRANTS: _____

PRIZE CATEGORIES   PRIZES

80s

FULL-SIZE WORKSHEET ON PAGE WS-46

"NYM" CENTER

MEET THE "NYMS"

Baby Syno-NYM is a copycat. When you say little, she says tiny, or wee, or microscopic.

Mrs. Anto-NYM always argues. If you say up, she says down. If you say right, she says wrong.

Mr. Homo-NYM always sounds the same. It's the meaning that is tricky, that's how he plays his game. When he says see, does he mean 🐝🐝 or 〰️〰️?

AT THIS CENTER YOU CAN:

1. Make a family tree of antonyms. Place one word on the trunk and all the antonym family members on the branches.
2. Rewrite a paragraph from a story. Substitute as many synonyms for words as you can.
3. Make up worksheets for your classmates. Ask your teacher to duplicate copies for you to pass out.
4. Prepare a lesson to teach on homonyms, antonyms, or synonyms.
5. Make up a book of silly homonyms with illustrations.

"Patience, patients."

"What a feat, feet!"

ANTONYMS

HOMONYMS

SYNONYMS

SYNONYM CONCENTRATION

SYNONYMS

DICTIONARY THESAURUS DICTIONARY

LEARNING POSSIBILITIES

Broadening oral and written vocabulary usage

Recognizing the meaning of synonym, homonym, and antonym

Knowing the appropriate use of synonyms, homonyms, and antonyms

Using dictionaries and thesauri

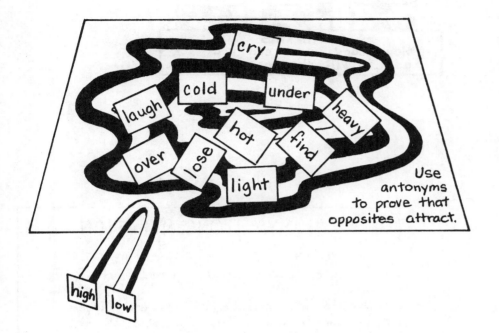

Use antonyms to prove that opposites attract.

GAMES AND ACTIVITIES

1. Write pairs of antonyms on cards, placing one word on each card. Put a paper clip on each card. Children take turns using a magnet to pick up the words which form the antonym pair.

2. Make the game board out of heavy cardboard. Use two library pockets to hold the cards during play. The envelope on the back is filled with pairs of antonym cards. One word is placed on each card.

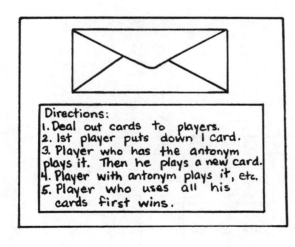

Directions:
1. Deal out cards to players.
2. 1st player puts down 1 card.
3. Player who has the antonym plays it. Then he plays a new card.
4. Player with antonym plays it, etc.
5. Player who uses all his cards first wins.

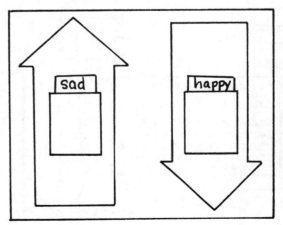

3. Paste a word on each can. Cut small cards to put with the game. Children find a synonym, write it on the card, and drop it into the can. Dictionaries and thesauri are helpful for locating words.

4. Make pairs of synonym cards and place them in an envelope. Write directions for playing the game on the envelope.

5. Make several different antonym-o cards. Vary the position of the words on the cards or vary the words used on the cards. Write antonyms for these words on small cards (one per card). Place these materials and markers to cover the words in a container with directions for playing the game.

SYNONYMS
How many words can you add to fill the cans up?

SYNONYM CONCENTRATION

Directions: Players: 2-4
1. Shuffle cards and spread out face down.
2. Decide who will be 1st, 2nd, etc. players.
3. 1st player turns up 2 cards. If they are synonyms he takes them. If not, he turns them face down again.
4. Each player, in turn, tries to match two synonyms.
5. The game is played until all cards are paired.

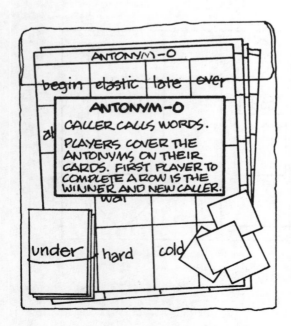

ANTONYM-O

CALLER CALLS WORDS.

PLAYERS COVER THE ANTONYMS ON THEIR CARDS. FIRST PLAYER TO COMPLETE A ROW IS THE WINNER AND NEW CALLER.

ANTONYM-O			
happy	over	high	before
lose	late	ahead	laugh
begin	FREE	elastic	hard
cold	success	war	slowly

WORKSHEETS

Name_____ Date_____

Fill the garden with synonym flowers. How many can you grow?

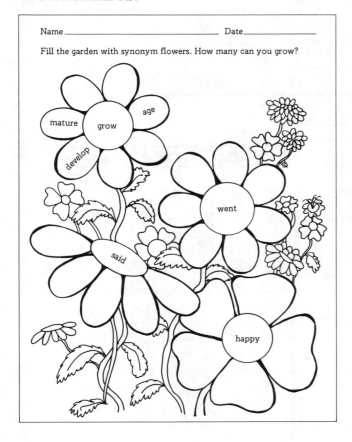

mature grow age

develop

went

said

happy

Name_____ Date_____

REWRITE the story.
Use synonyms to replace the underlined words.

One day a <u>little</u> boy was <u>walking</u> down the <u>street</u>. He <u>saw</u> a coin lying on the sidewalk.

He <u>looked</u> all around but <u>saw</u> no one. So he bent down and <u>picked up</u> the coin.

He <u>wanted</u> to <u>find out</u> who it belonged to, so he <u>started</u> <u>going</u> to the houses nearby.

Finally, the boy <u>found</u> the person who had <u>lost</u> the coin. The person <u>gave</u> him a reward for returning the coin.

Now. . .write your own story. Underline the synonyms. Give it to a friend to replace the underlined words.

_____
_____
_____
_____
_____
_____
_____
_____
_____
_____
_____
_____
_____
_____
_____
_____
_____
_____
_____

Name _____ Date _____
Name _____

YOU DON'T SAY

You'll need two people for this worksheet. Take a part, YOU SAY or I SAY, and fill in the blanks on your half of the page by writing an antonym for the word underlined in the other person's part. Help each other fill in the blanks. When you have completed the page, read lines to each other emphasizing the underlined words.

I SAY	YOU SAY
1. Let's <u>go</u>.	No, let's _____.
2. I _____ you.	I <u>love</u> you.
3. I like _____ carrots.	I like them <u>raw</u>.
4. I <u>found</u> my roller skate key.	Did you? I just _____ mine.
5. The parking lot is _____.	There's another one that is <u>empty</u>.
6. I think this is a <u>private</u> beach.	No, look at the sign, it says _____.
7. Are we heading _____?	We're traveling <u>south</u>.
8. I <u>forgot</u> to bring home the bacon.	Don't worry. I _____.
9. What a _____ drive.	I think it's very <u>interesting</u>.
10. Don't those flowers look <u>real</u>?	Yes, but I think they're_____.

Select one <u>pair</u> of sentences. Write a continuous dialogue for 2 people using the lines you selected as their first lines. Use as many antonyms as you can in your script.

Name _____ Date _____

For this game you will need:

| a friend | a pencil |
| a die | 2 markers (a penny or scrap of paper will do) |

To play:
1. Decide which path each of you will take.
2. Roll the die. Move the number of spaces shown on the die.
3. Follow the directions in the square you land on.
4. If your answer(s) is correct, roll the die again to determine your points. Keep a running tally of your score.

The winner is the player with the largest total number of points at the end of the game.

QUEUE up on CUE.
Wait here during your next turn.

WRITE TWO HOMONYMS FOR SEES.

Will you
P
a P
of P___s?

SAIL ON to the SALE SALE. Move ahead 3 and subtract 3 points.

CENSE means to perfume w/incense
Write 3 homonyms for it.
1.
2.
3.

WRITE A SENTENCE USING ILL, AISLE and ISLE.

THEIR biking over THEY'RE with THERE lunches.
REWRITE THIS SENTENCE CORRECTLY.

Who ate the

donut.

and all?

Player 1

START

FLEA, FLEE!
Move back one.

Don't WAVER! you just received your WAIVER Move ahead 2!

FLEE, FLEA! move back one.

I've brought apples you. You've WON! Move ahead ONE!

WRITE TWO HOMONYMS FOR he'll

Would bags be + heavy + carry?

TOO hot! Wait here for two turns.

The pirate on the SEES, SEIZE the loot and will SEAS it.
REWRITE THIS SENTENCE CORRECTLY.

USE road, rowed, and rode in a sentence.

Player 2

START

SHOOT down the CHUTE! Move ahead 3 and subtract 3 points.

A P of an olive branch is a symbol for P____.

Writing

AT THIS CENTER YOU CAN:

1. Add a sample of a famous person's handwriting to the class autograph book.
2. Make an alphabet chart to show the letters and script of a foreign language.
3. Use copy-editing symbols to proofread one of the stories you have written.
4. Select four quotes from Bartlett's and use them as dialogue for a character in an imaginary story.
5. Make a list of all the things each member of your family writes in one day.

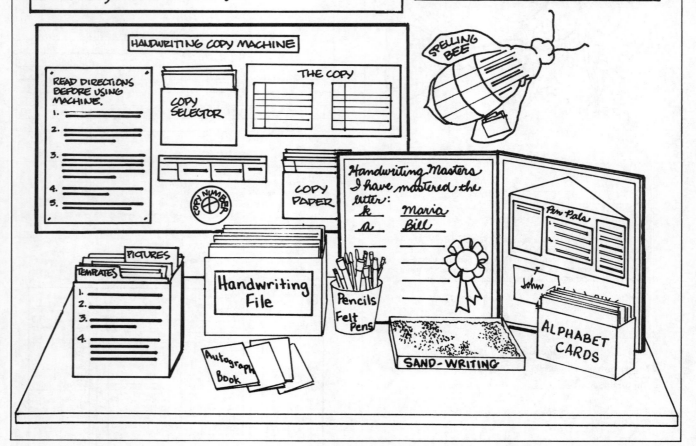

LEARNING POSSIBILITIES

Stimulating various forms of creative writing

Introducing and applying proofreading skills

Practicing handwriting skills, such as slant, closing loops, capitals, and writing on the line

Applying understanding of spelling rules

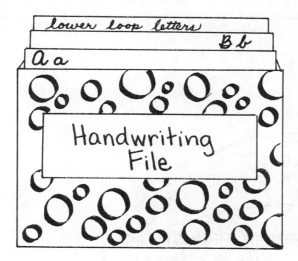

GAMES AND ACTIVITIES

1. Fill the lid of a heavy box half full with sand. Students practice writing letters or words in the sand. Students can be instructed to copy onto paper the "best" letter or word they have practiced in the sand.

2. Make a handwriting file that contains worksheets grouped according to a skill or a specific letter. Label dividers to show the skill or letter for each section of the file. Children select the worksheets they need to practice.

3. Collect a variety of 8½ x 11 colored pictures. Make a set of templates by cutting out shapes and labeling them with elements related to various types of stories. Children select a template and picture, place the template over the picture, and use what shows through the template as the basis for starting their own story.

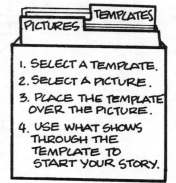

4. Construct a large pen pal envelope for use on a bulletin board or table top. The writing forms on the Postage Due list can be changed to match the curriculum or students' needs and interests. Encourage pen pals to maintain communication by using a different writing form each time they correspond with one another.

5. Make a set of correctly and incorrectly spelled word cards. Children select a word card, classify it as correct or incorrect, and match it to the appropriate spelling rule. The Spelling Bee chart should be constructed so that many words can be matched to each spelling rule. The spelling rules used on the chart can be changed to correspond with the spelling curriculum and/or students' needs and interests.

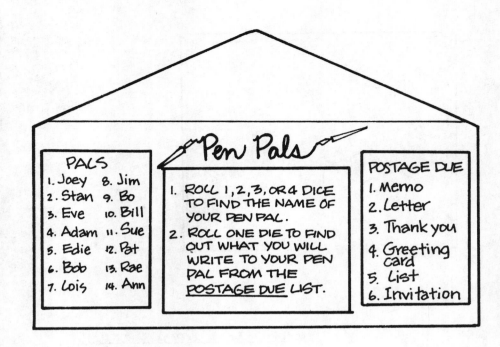

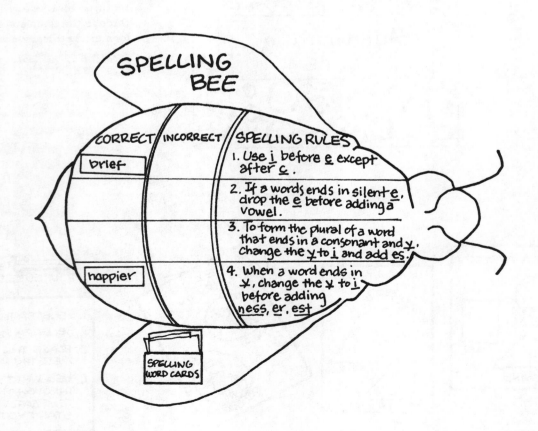

6. Children select a partner and decide which member of the team will be the writer and which will be the proofreader. They move through the calendar by rolling a die. Each date on the calendar describes a task for the writer and indicates a task for the proofreader. The proofreader's task is represented by a pattern that is keyed to the border of the calendar. The writer completes the written task and gives it to the proofreader to correct. One point is subtracted from the date for each error the proofreader finds. The winning team is the one with the most points at the time the playing period ends.

TALLY CARD

DATE _____
WRITER _____
PROOFREADER
_____

DATE	ERRORS	TOTAL

PROOFREAD FOR CAPITALS

PROOFREAD FOR SPELLING

PROOFREAD FOR LEGIBILITY

PROOFREAD FOR PUNCTUATION

Writing and Proofreading CALENDAR FOR DECEMBER

1 INVITATION	2 RECIPE	3 ITINERARY	4 POEM	5 DIRECTIONS	6 LIST
7 MINUTES OF A MEETING	8 Pencil broke, rest today.	9 CAPTION	10 RIDDLE	11 PHONE MESSAGE	12 BROCHURE	13 Change noted. Roll again to find out what to do.
14 HEADLINES	15 SHORT STORY	16 PROGRAM	17 LETTER	18 NEWS ARTICLE	19 GREETING CARD	20 INTERVIEW
21 AD	22 LETTER	23 SCHEDULE	24 MEMO	25 SET OF RULES	26 Writer's cramp. Rest today.	27 A PARAGRAPH
28 REVIEW	29 REPORT	30 PLAN	31 NOTE			

7. Set up the copy machine on a bulletin board. Collect printed poems, captions, etc., for children to transpose into cursive writing. Review the directions for using the Handwriting Copy Machine with the children.

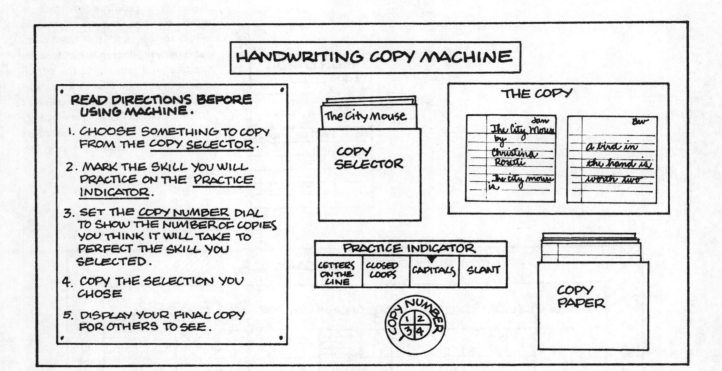

WORKSHEETS

Name _____ Date _____

HANDWRITING SCORE SHEET

Rules | Write sentences or a paragraph here: | Score

2 points for all letters on line

1 point for closing letters a, d, g

3 points for even slant / / / /

2 points for <u>even</u> height arm

2 points for not looping these letters d, t, i

Total Score _____

Name _____ Date _____

TRACE-PRACTICE-PERFECT

1. Choose a letter to practice.

2. Have the teacher write it for you.

3. Trace the letter as many times as you need to.

Trace   Practice   Write your perfect letter

FULL-SIZE WORKSHEET ON PAGE WS-49

Name _____ Date _____

PROOFREADING CHECKPOINTS

Write a story.
　　　at each stop sign.
　　Check what you have written for what is posted on the stop sign before you continue your story.

Title: _____

STOP! Check for . , ?

STOP! Check for legibility.

STOP! Check for spelling.

STOP! Check capitals.

Name _____ Date _____

Jot·a·story

Jot down your first response to each of these items.

an adjective describing you		a verb describing a funny movement	
a noun describing an imaginary object		an adverb describing an awkward movement	
a color	a season	a place	a favorite thing

Use all or as many of the responses you have jotted down in one sentence.

Use the sentence you just jotted down as the first sentence in your story. Jot down the rest of your story here.

FULL-SIZE WORKSHEET ON PAGE WS-50

4
Record Keeping and Evaluation

RECORD KEEPING AND EVALUATION

Record keeping cannot be separated from evaluation. Record keeping tells what has been accomplished, and evaluation tells how well it has been accomplished.

Record keeping and evaluation are a continuous process which involves the student and the teacher in accounting, considering, and reporting individual growth and learning progress. The devices used for record keeping and evaluation indicate which tasks the student has undertaken, how much he has accomplished, and how successful he has been. These records not only show what the student has done, but also help in planning for future learnings.

The teacher and the student share the responsibilities for maintaining the records. They also decide which instruments and procedures to employ.

THE IMPORTANCE OF RECORD KEEPING

For the Parent: Records form a comprehensive picture of the student's activities in the classroom.

For the Student: Record keeping develops the child's responsibility for charting and following through on a course of study. It provides the child with a feeling of accomplishment and an identity as a learner. The record-keeping process also helps students to see many possibilities for learning.

For the Teacher: Records supply the teacher with a permanent accounting of what the student has been doing, and thus allow the teacher to further plan and provide for the student. Records are a reference for interpreting pupil progress to parents.

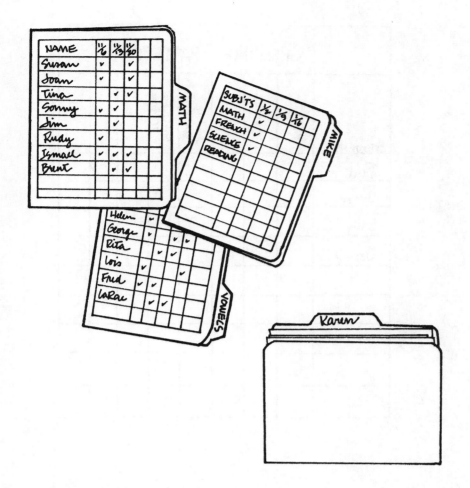

METHODS OF ORGANIZING RECORDS FOR THE TEACHER

Records can be organized several ways to make them easily accessible and usable. A folder can be kept for each subject, for each child, or for each group. A checklist on the front shows who has had conferences with the teacher and who still needs to be seen.

Sample Work File

The teacher retains several samples of work from each subject area. This file may then be used in conferencing to observe current work or, if collected over a longer period of time, progress of work.

Total Class Record

This chart, showing the dates mastery was achieved in various skills, is kept by the teacher. At a glance, the teacher can see the need for specific skill groups and the children who should be in the groups. For example, Mary, Karen, and Tommy might be part of a group to learn addition with regrouping. Both charts can be used to keep records of the computational skills mastered.

	Add without regrouping	Add with regrouping	Column addition	
JOHN A.	9/27	9/30	10/30	
MARY	9/30	10/7		
BETH	9/30		9/30	
STAN D.	9/30	10/30	11/30	
TOMMY	9/30			
KAREN	9/30		10/15	

Spelling Patterns

This record-keeping instrument focuses on the structural rules related to learning how to spell. The teacher fills in the headings after determining the rules which are most appropriate for her class. A check next to a student's name indicates that he has learned to apply the rule.

Spelling Assessment Sheet

This instrument helps the teacher determine each student's ability to apply spelling skills, to learn new words, and to use spelling words in written context. The teacher assesses each student according to subjective and objective methods.

STUDENTS	SPELLING PATTERNS							
	short vowels	silent e	endings	double consonants	suffixes, prefixes			
Paul								
Jean								
Sally L.								
Jerry								

SPELLING / VOCABULARY DEVELOPMENT			
Needs basic words often	Asks for new words	Looks up own words	Attempts to spell phonetically

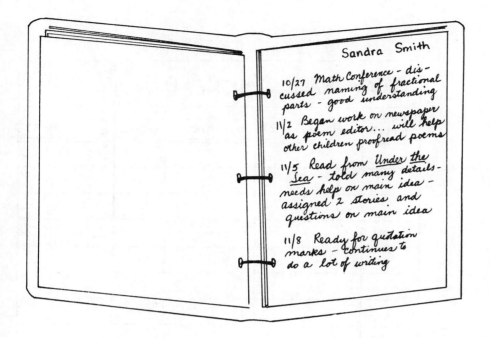

Anecdotal Records Notebook

This notebook can be used by the teacher for recording information gathered in conferences and from observations. Records can be used to plan skill groups, report to parents, and show ongoing progress during the year.

Conference Record

This sample is a method of recording each child's conferences with the teacher throughout the year. Any code may be developed to meet a teacher's needs. The circled letters indicate conferences that have already been held. The empty circles indicate conferences the teacher or child plan to have. At a glance, the teacher can see children she has not conferenced with recently. The record sheet can act as a reminder for writing anecdotal records at the end of the day or week.

Notebook page reads:

Sandra Smith

10/27 Math Conference - discussed naming of fractional parts - good understanding

11/2 Began work on newspaper as poem editor... will help other children proofread poems

11/5 Read from Under the Sea - told many details - needs help on main idea - assigned 2 stories and questions on main idea

11/8 Ready for quotation marks - continues to do a lot of writing

	10/20	10/21	10/22	10/23	10/24				
Tom B.	Ⓜ				ᴹ◯				
Sharon C.		Ⓡ							
David F.			Ⓡ						
Mary J.			ᴿ⊗						
George L.		Ⓡ,Ⓟ	ᴹ◯						

Ⓜ = Math Conference held

Ⓟ = Proofreading Conference held

Ⓡ = Reading Conference held

ᴹ◯ = indicates Math Conference is needed circle is "X'd" when Conference is completed

RECORD KEEPING FOR THE STUDENT

My Library and What Have You Read?

Either page may be used by individual children as a personal reading record. These records may be kept in a notebook, a file box, or a pocket chart at the reading center, or each child may keep his own sheet or card in his reading or work folder. These pages provide a basis of information to help the teacher schedule small-group instruction according to needs and interests.

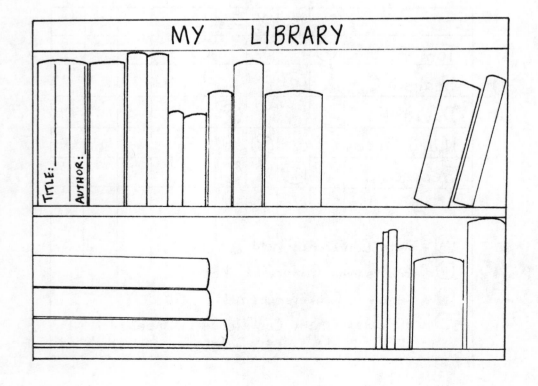

WHAT HAVE YOU READ?

Date Started	Title of Book	Author	Date Finished	Comments

MY LIBRARY

TITLE: _____
AUTHOR: _____

The second example of "My Library" shows how a record-keeping sheet can be added to include evaluating.

MY LIBRARY

TITLE _Sarah in Story_
AUTHOR _2. Wylie_ _nonfiction_

TITLE _Blue Willow_
AUTHOR _Doris Gates_ _fiction_

TITLE _Saw the Sarah_
AUTHOR _B. Miller_ _nonfiction_

TITLE ___The Borrowers___
AUTHOR ___Mary Norton___ _fiction_

TITLE _____
AUTHOR _____

NAME _Kristin_
WEEK OF _February 8_
I read _2 non-fiction books and 2 fiction books_.
_____

The 3 major differences between them are ____
_____
_____

Reading Circles

The teacher identifies the skill areas the students will learn and the activities they will do. Coloring over a part of each circle indicates what the student has accomplished.

Individual Record

Each child has a card. The cards for the class may be kept in a three-ring notebook or in a filebox at the math center, or each child may keep his own in his math folder. The child records the date of the test or conference when mastery of the skill is achieved.

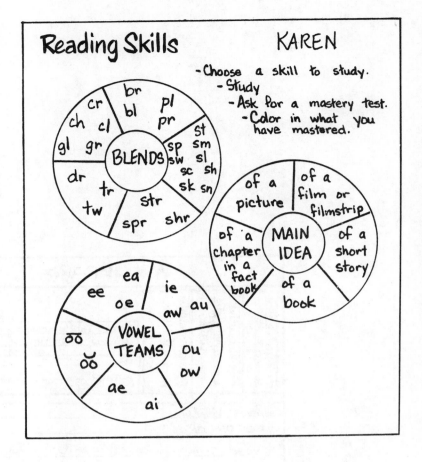

I KNOW...				
the basic addition facts				
the basic subtraction facts				
the basic multiplication facts				
the basic division facts				
I CAN...				
add without regrouping				
add with regrouping				
add columns of numbers				
subtract without regrouping				
subtract with regrouping				

Spelling Box

Each pupil maintains a spelling box to keep track of the words she is studying and the words she has learned. The words in the section labeled "Words I Know" can be used as a source for developing a review spelling list. Students can exchange words to form their new spelling lists.

Spelling Scroll

The student shows that he has learned a spelling word by using it in his monthly story. The scroll keeps track of words learned and shows the student's ability to use words in their proper context. A comparison of monthly stories will provide evidence of the student's progress in spelling and writing.

Balloon

Each child writes the skill he will be studying on a balloon and colors it yellow. He recolors the balloon with a red crayon when he has mastered the skill. An orange balloon signifies that the child has learned that skill and is ready to tackle a new one.

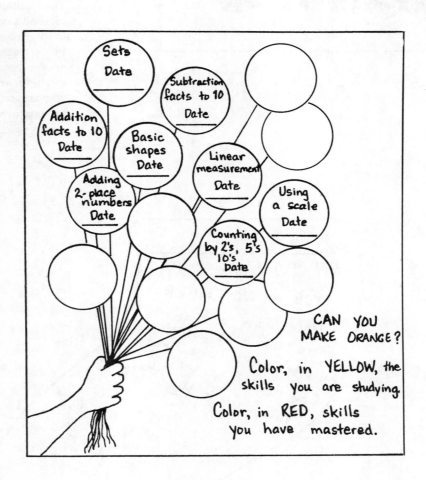

Date 4-10	Skill being studied periods	Activity	Written work	Mastery

Name _Dolores_

Activity Cut and paste · Writing · Mastery

Cut and Paste

A student cuts the symbol which indicates his level of progress from the bottom of the page. The symbol is pasted into the appropriate column on the ditto and the activity and date are entered.

Writing Sampler

The teacher and the student define the skill that needs to be developed from the student's own writing. A sample which shows the deficient skill is cut and pasted onto a page in the sampler. A sample showing the student's progress is later cut and pasted on the same page. This sheet combines record keeping and evaluation.

MY Writing Sampler

Date: 2-17-71
Skill: even spacing

1st sample

The magic flower grew until it reached the roof-tops

Improved sample

The rocket ship had a silvery, shiny look. It was

Language Study Box

The teacher surveys basic curriculum or class interests and abilities to determine the language areas to be emphasized. These areas become headings for the dividers in the record-keeping box. Each child has a card or cards which identify his learning need(s) and his progress. The cards are filed behind the subject area in which he is working.

My Writing Book

Each student has his own writing book, which contains all of his writings. It helps the teacher and student to diagnose the student's needs and is a continuous record of communication between the teacher and the student.

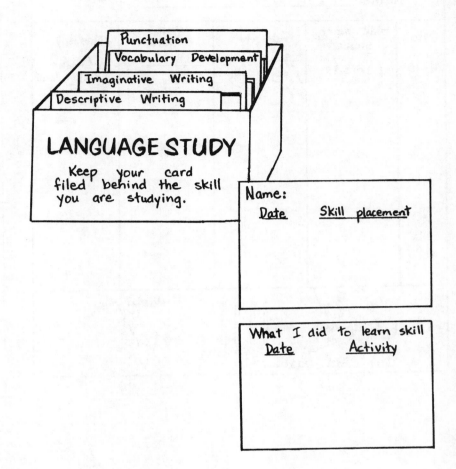

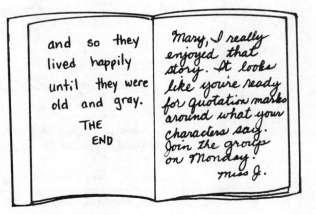

NAME ✓ CHECKING UP ON WHAT I'VE DONE	WEEK OF				
✱ daily "musts"	MON.	TUES.	WED.	THURS.	FRI.
✱ Math Activity					
Independent Study					
Story or poem writing					
✱ Reading					
Handwriting					
Art or Music					
✱ Measurement or Cooking Center					
Animal Stories or Magnets Center					

Checking Up

Students are required to do the daily musts which have been filled in by the teacher. They complete the rest of their weekly schedule according to their own choices. Students then check off what they have done.

Key Chain

A different colored key is designated for each working area. After working in an area, the student fills out a key and adds it to his key chain. In this way he keeps a record of what he did during the day or week. Adding keys to his key chain gives the student a sense of accomplishment and enables the teacher to see how he utilized his time.

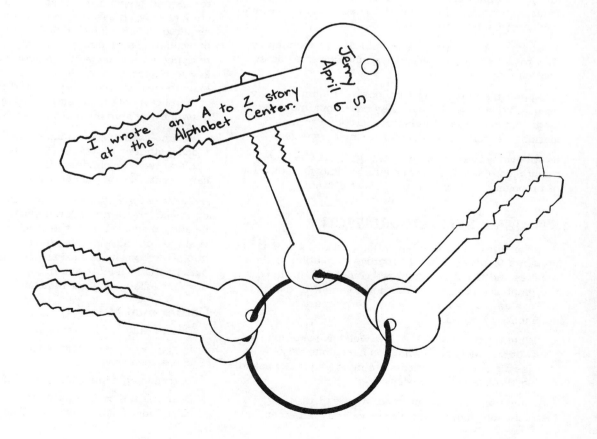

LOOKING AT LEARNING OUTCOMES

Evaluation can be seen as the process of judging, formally or informally, the merit or worth of outcomes of the teaching/learning process, such as student performance and teaching materials and methods.

Teachers have their own methods of evaluating student performance; however, the following suggestions may be useful as evaluative techniques for learning-center work.

1. Teacher-made pre- and post-tests, based on learning-center objectives, can be placed at a center or can be given to students before working and again after a given amount of work has been completed at the center.

Many of the Learning Possibilities that accompany each learning center in this book can be adapted to specific behavioral objectives. For centers that contain a wide range of activities or cover several related skills, brief tests or assessing procedures may be used to determine whether a child moves on to more advanced parts of the center.

2. Students may be asked to demonstrate, with a selection of learning-center materials, mastery of skills and content during a teacher-student conference.

3. A checklist based on individual criteria or competencies may be used periodically by the teacher during informal observation of a student or group of students working, or may be combined with more formal testing or conference methods.

4. Children may suggest and help design techniques that would show mastery of learning-center skills and content.

5. Applicable portions of textbooks and commercially prepared test or worksheets may be cut out, mounted on cards, laminated for durability, and coded to match learning centers or portions of learning centers.

6. An evaluative comment or checklist may be added to many record-keeping instruments to lend an indication of proficiency in skills or mastery of content.

STUDENT SELF-EVALUATION

Another purpose of the evaluation process is to enable students to perceive their progress in relation to their abilities and the work they have completed. In this case the emphasis is more on the development of habits of self-evaluation than on absolute correctness in comments recorded.

"What have you done?" "How well have you done it?" "How do you feel about what you have done?" These are the questions which students are most frequently asked during the evaluation process.

Evaluation must be an integral part of the instructional program and the school day. The teacher's responsibility is to plan the method and time for evaluation and to teach the students how to evaluate. The type of evaluation used is dependent on the student and the learning activity and may be either oral or written.

Evaluating Academic Growth

The evaluation tool designed for measuring cognitive or academic growth may ask for either a subjective or an objective response. The student's progress may be recorded intermittently or consistently over a period of time.

Evaluating Personal Growth

The basic tool for this type of evaluation is primarily the subjective type, which allows the student to express his feelings freely. The student's attitudes about school and his work are included in this affective type of evaluation. Evaluation of the student's self-concept helps him to answer, "Who am I?"

EVALUATION CONFERENCE

The evaluation method which provides the greatest opportunity for student-teacher interaction is the evaluation conference. It is structured to give the students a chance to share their accomplishments and their feelings concerning them. This time is spent in dialogue, which allows *both* the teacher and the student to ask and respond to questions and concerns. The student may be asked to demonstrate her newly acquired skills or knowledge. The most beneficial means of evaluating such student progress is to ask the student to apply her learnings in a new or different context. The key to a successful evaluation conference is to provide enough time to *share, discuss,* and *react.* An evaluation conference implies shared leadership and responsibility between the student and the teacher.

A time-saving way to adapt the individual teacher-student conference is to hold small-group conferences with children who have been working at the same center or on similar skills.

Another type of small-group conference is based on a curricular area, and children share learnings and skills recently mastered with the teacher and group. For example, during a reading-group conference, each child brings the book he or she has been reading, selects a few paragraphs to read to the group, and shares any center or other follow-up work that has been completed.

Conference Musts

Designating a conference period or block of time

Designing a method for children to sign up for a conference time

Determining a place for the conference

Deciding the standards which other students in the class must follow while the teacher is conferencing

Indicating to the students what is to be brought to the conference

Reminding children to prepare questions they wish to ask.

It should be reiterated that any learning center built around specified objectives can be evaluated in formal behavioral objective terms. If a letter-grading system, point system, or grading curve is used by the teacher, requirements for earning grades and points for center work need to be clearly established with students.

SELF-EVALUATIONS OF ACADEMIC AND SOCIAL GROWTH

Measuring Up

This self-evaluation tool may be used by the student for assessing any or all learning experiences. A time designated for evaluation reinforces the importance of doing this type of activity.

Diary

Students may keep a diary to record their feelings about a particular learning activity or about the experiences of the entire school day.

HOW DO I MEASURE UP?

Date: _____

I wanted to accomplish:
_____
_____
_____

What I did:
_____
_____
_____
_____
_____

How I feel about what I did:
_____
_____
_____
_____
_____
_____

MY DIARY

11/16 — I finished my project on Cars today. I'm happy with it, especially the drawings. I wish I could have typed up the information.

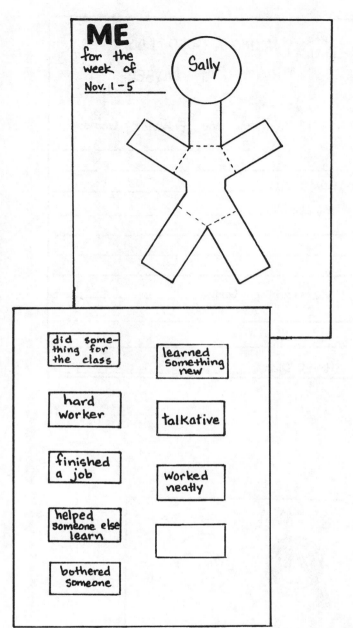

Me

The child draws his face onto the figure. At the close of each school week, he selects the characteristic which best describes him for that week. He cuts and pastes this onto the stick figure. The completed figure provides an accounting of the child's feeling about himself or his work.

Evaluation Bulletin Board

Divide a bulletin board into several sections, depending on your needs for evaluation. Make up several name tags for each child and pin to one side of the board.

Before going home for the day, each child attaches his name tags to locations on the board, indicating how the child sees his performance for that day. At the beginning of the next day, the teacher or a monitor repins the tags to the side portion of the board. The teacher may periodically record (by a class checklist, individual student record sheet, or by photograph) a day's completed bulletin board and compare it from week to week, or month to month.

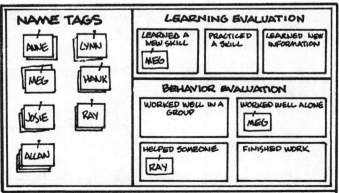

Taking a Look at Myself

Effective with older children, this worksheet helps to differentiate the types of goals students can have as they work in the classroom. These goals can be related to a particular learning activity or to a given period of time within the school week. This type of device encourages a student to be responsible for his own learning and behavior.

Continuum

This instrument presents students with examples of behavior. Each behavior is shown with its opposite. Students are to place a mark on the continuum to indicate what they feel their behavior is most like. This can be filled out before and after a given period. In this way the student can compare how he expects to behave with his actual behavior.

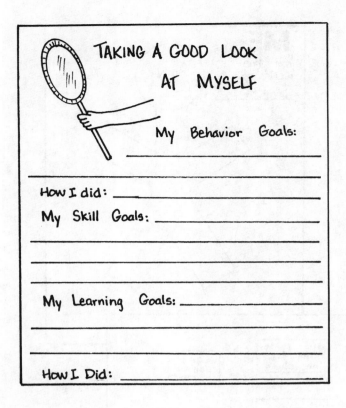

THIS IS _John W._

MY GOALS: I want to ex-
periment to see which kind
of soil grows the best plants.
I want to learn to play
the autoharp.
I want to do better at not
bothering others when they're working.

MY RECENT ACCOMPLISHMENTS:
I finished my seed-sprouting
experiments.
I've really improved my
cursive writing.
I learned to multiply
and divide 2-place
numbers.
I haven't been in a
fight for 1 month.

DATE: Dec. 1

Profile

Each child makes a profile of himself. In an individual conference
with the teacher, learning or behavioral goals are set for the student. He records these on his profile. After a designated period of
time, the student also records his
accomplishments.

Take-Home Reports

At the end of the school day, children fill out a Take-Home Report
worksheet summarizing their activities and evaluation of those activities. The form is taken home to
share with parents. Parents may
be asked to respond in a section of
the form, which is then torn off and
returned to school the next day.

Older children may fill out the
form themselves. Younger children may need the help of an aide,
older child, or teacher. Due to time
limitations, one designated group
of children may complete the form
each day. In this case each child
may only take home one report per
week.

TODAY

_____
(date)

I had a
☐ great day
☐ good day
☐ so-so day
☐ difficult day

Something I learned today:

insects have 6 legs

Tonight I need to:

complete Math, page 36

Some of my activities were:

• made a graph

• began a new library book

My child and I: read together

Mr. Laney
(parent signat.)
(return to school)

5
Planning Classroom Time

PLANNING CLASSROOM TIME

Planning is an important aspect of the total day for both the teacher and the child. It can be used to schedule activities and learning-center time regardless of the organization of the classroom. Learning centers can be used all day as a total approach to education or for only an hour a day, after other work is completed, as a part of multiple-group reading, or in any other way to fit in with existing classroom organization. The teacher decides which is the best way for his or her class.

Planning should be considered individually for each child. One child may be able to plan and follow a schedule a whole week while another may be self-directed enough only to schedule one hour at a time. This same self-directedness and independence may characterize one reading group but not another. Also, the child who could only schedule an hour a day one week may be able to add a second hour the next week. Thus, individuality and flexibility are other important aspects of planning.

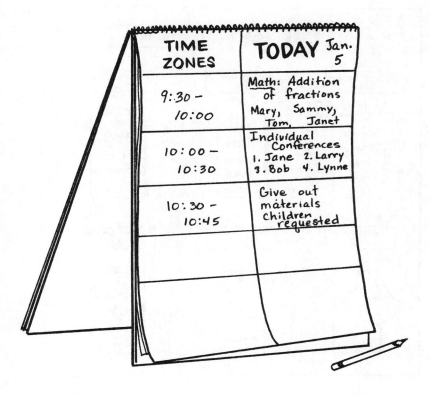

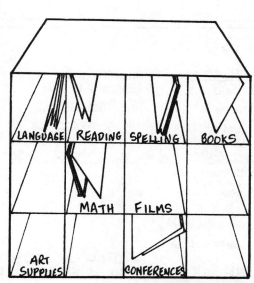

THE TEACHER'S DAY

Who needs my help?

What skills or subjects need to be taught?

What must I do to motivate interest in a center or subject?

The teacher's answers to these questions will determine how he structures his day, interacting with groups and individuals. His daily routine must allow time for teaching and for engaging in dialogue and intervention with students. For efficient planning and scheduling, the teacher must competently assess the class needs and assign priorities for his time on the basis of these needs.

The teacher's schedule should always be a flexible outline of activities. Leaving empty blocks of time allows the teacher freedom to work with students as their needs arise.

Chart Planning

A teacher may use a large spiral tablet to communicate with students, informing the class of what will be done at various times during the school day. This method allows the teacher flexibility in planning each day according to the students' changing needs.

Slot Planning

Students record their needs and interests on cards. These cards are placed into slots which have been labeled for different subject or activity areas. The teacher surveys the cards at the end of each day or week and uses them as a reference in planning time and activities for the class.

Today

Pads of paper clipped or hooked onto pieces of wood or cardboard form charts which can be used to announce the teacher's schedule for the day. Activity and time headings are written on slips of paper which are slipped into precut slots above each pad. Students sign up for the activities on the pads of paper.

Chalkboard

The teacher fills in the chalkboard outline with the class at the beginning of the school day. This type of planning is a quick and efficient method of indicating what the teacher has planned for certain students. It is also a way of communicating the learning possibilities available to the class.

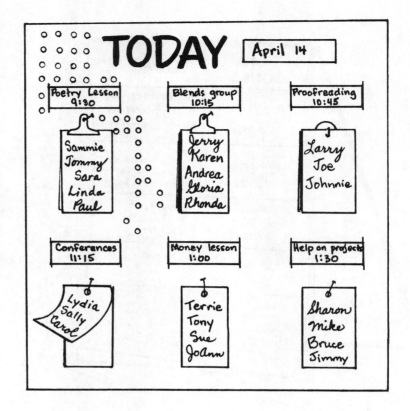

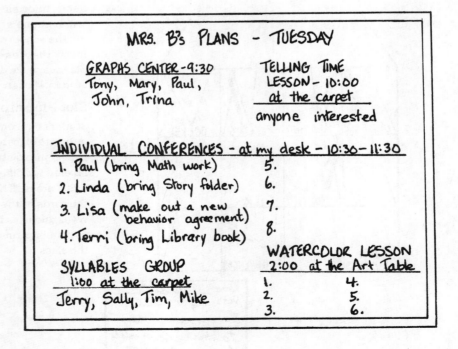

GETTING THE STUDENT INTO MOTION

The purpose of any planning device is to provide the student with a tool that will help her become an independent and responsible learner and increase her awareness of her abilities and interests. The use of any planning device should enable the student to develop a self-directedness which can be applied in and out of the classroom.

Planning devices provide students with formats that assist them in budgeting their time, programming their learnings, and making decisions from the choice of activities available to them. The type of schedule used depends on the teacher's intent and the students' needs and capabilities. All of the devices offer students a range of choices.

Planning devices may help students to determine:

WHAT? the activity they select from the alternatives available to them

WHEN? the sequence of the activities they will do within a period or block of time

HOW? the means they will use to perform the activities they have chosen

WHERE? the place they will work

Any or all of these points may be incorporated into a planning device.

ROTATIONAL SCHEDULING

Groups of children are rotated to learning activities. In this type of scheduling, students do not decide when they will go to the activity or center, but rather what they will do when they get to that activity.

Circle Planning

The experiences which the teacher thinks are imperative for students are written on the outer circle. The teacher controls the sequence of places where students work by rotating the inner circle during the day, or she can change it at the beginning of each day and instruct the students to do each activity by moving clockwise.

Revolving Reading

The teacher divides the children into four groups. Each group begins the schedule as shown and proceeds when the teacher directs it. This plan could be utilized in a four-group reading program or when planning for a single-subject area only.

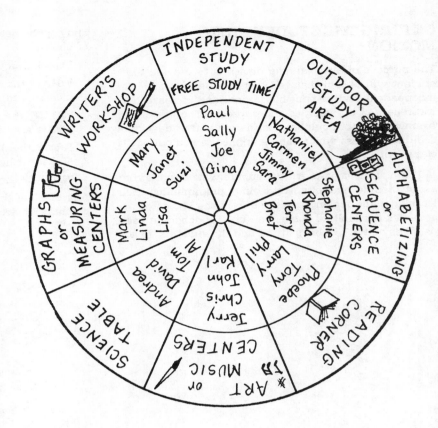

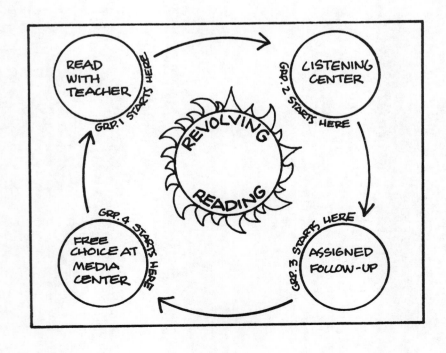

Oct. 6

Dear Sally
A reminder to:

— Finish your Insect
Collection
— Do 3 graphs
— Practice capital letters
in cursive writing
— Do 2 activities from
the Tall Tales Center
— Help Joan with her
multiplication work
Mrs. S.

Return to
sender by:
Oct. 14
Mrs. S: I have...

ASSIGNMENTS

Children are assigned to activities or centers according to diagnosed needs. They may choose *when* to go to the assigned area and/or *what* to do at the assigned area.

Postcard

The teacher and students can design their own postcards. These act as personalized communications between the teacher and the student. They inform the student of the tasks that have been assigned to him. The student returns the postcards to relate his accomplishments.

Cut and Paste Schedule

Assignments for the total class are written in some of the geometric shapes on the ditto by the teacher. The extra shapes are filled in by the teacher and/or student for individualized assignments. When the student completes an assignment, he cuts out the shape on which the assignment was written and pastes it on the other side of the ditto.

CUT AND PASTE
AS YOU FINISH
YOUR WORK

CUT HERE

Visit
Writer's
Workshop

Do
3
measuring
activities

Read a
library book
Do a book
sharing
activity.

THINGS I'VE
DONE

PASTE
HERE

CONTRACTING

Students develop an agreement which states their choices of what to do, when to do it, and how to do it.

Learning Contract

Students contract with the teacher to get involved in a learning experience or to perform a specific task. This contract should be developed cooperatively and the terms must be clearly understood by the student. Before signing the contract, he must know the time allotted to complete the work and the consequences if he fails to fulfill the contract.

My Plans

The plans made for the total class are dittoed. The open time blocks are filled in by the student. The schedule is considered to be a contractual agreement when it is initialed by both the teacher and the student. The student's initials signify her commitment to fulfill her plans. The teacher's initials signify her approval of the student's program.

MY PLANS — Paul W.

	MONDAY	TUESDAY	WEDNESDAY	THURSDAY	FRIDAY
	Opening / Planning time				
9:15-9:45	ASSEMBLY			Film	
9:45-10:15	ASSEMBLY				
10:15	RECESS				
10:30-11:30		Visit Library		Neighborhood Walk	
11:30	LUNCH				
12:30-1:30	Animal Stories Group	Tall Tales Group	Animal Stories Group	Tall Tales Group	
1:30	PHYSICAL EDUCATION				
2:00-2:30					Film
2:30	EVALUATION / CLEAN-UP				

Schedule O.K'd _____ student initials _____ teacher initials

My Plans Name_____	
Write a book	
Games	
Project	
Records, tapes	
Filmstrips	
Flashcards be w see	
Read a book	

SELF-PROGRAMMING

Students are given freedom to set their own courses of learning from those activities available in the environment. The teacher may initially allow only the independent students to program themselves while she works with others who are more dependent on teacher direction. The students may move from programming themselves for a small portion of each day to programming themselves for the entire day. The goal is for each student to find his own way to best use his time.

My Plans

Children select and number the activities in the order they will do them. Planning sheets which use pictures help primary students to make learning choices.

Planning Checklist

This planning sheet is designed to schedule children for a particular subject area and block of time. Listed are the learning choices for an individualized language arts program. The student checks where she is going to work. After completing the activity, the student places an X alongside her choice.

This device could easily be used for planning only one period a day or for a period after other work is completed.

	My Choice	I Completed
Art Center		
Alphabetizing Center		
Animal Center		
Go to the Library		
Read a book		
Vowel Center		
Write a story		
I can plan by myself. Name:		

Floor Plan

A diagram or model of the classroom is made. Each student places his flag on the area where he has chosen to work. This method of planning presents the students with an overview of all the learning possibilities which are available to them within the room. It also aids the teacher in keeping track of where students are working at a given time. The diagram can be charted and placed on a bulletin board, or it can be outlined with paint or masking tape on the classroom floor.

Must Planning

The teacher can control learning by presenting students with certain requirements for which they are responsible. Students write their own plans around the outside of the "musts." Each student is expected to schedule her time to include the "musts." But the student decides when to do them.

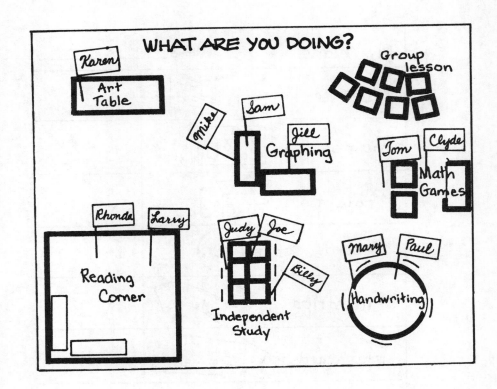

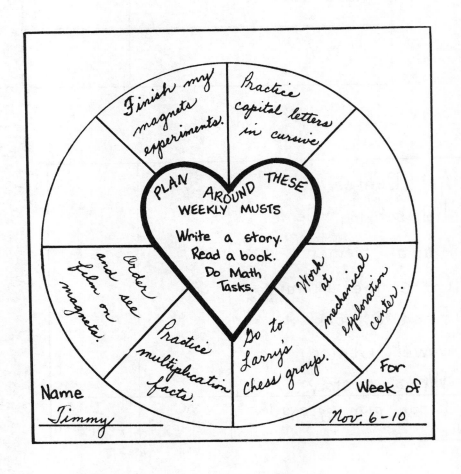

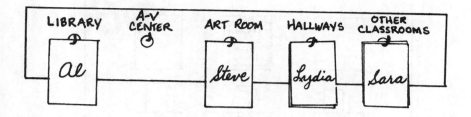

PLANNING FOR WORK OUTSIDE THE CLASSROOM AND SPECIAL EVENTS

Cup Hook Rack

A rack made of cup hooks inserted into a piece of lumber can be used to keep track of students who are working in areas outside the classroom. Students hang their name cards below the label of the place where they can be found.

Chalkboard

A small chalkboard is placed near a classroom door. Children sign out before leaving the room by writing their names and the areas to which they are going.

Clock Out

Each student is expected to record his name and the place where he will be working on a slip of paper. This is placed in the chart opposite the time he is leaving the room.

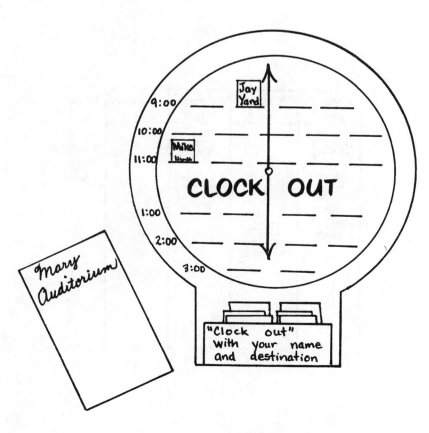

Special Happenings

Advertising special events is a means of introducing and motivating students to current happenings available to them. A sign is clipped over a pocket to announce the activity being presented. The students who wish to participate in the event sign up on strips of paper, which they place in the correctly labeled pocket on the chart. This process stimulates student involvement and commitment for the activity. The number of students who can be part of the event can also be regulated.

Acetate Overlay

The use of acetate or plastic over a master weekly schedule enables the teacher to reuse the chart each week. With crayon or grease pencil, the special events for the week are recorded for the students.

Monday May 1	Tuesday May 2	Wednesday May 3	Thursday May 4	Friday May 5
9:30 -Sewing 10:00 -African Slides -Bird Walk	11:00 Map Making	9:30 -Sewing 10:00 -African Slides		9:30 -Sewing -Rhythm Band

6
Independent Study

WHAT IS INDEPENDENT STUDY?

Defining Independent Study

Independent study is an individualized learning experience which allows the student to select a topic, define problems or questions, gather and analyze information, apply skills, and create a product to show what has been learned.

Purposes of Independent Study

Although the purposes of independent study can be generalized for all students, individual factors such as entry-level skills and interests will cause different purposes to be emphasized for different learners. The general purposes of an independent study include the following:

to develop self-directedness

to acquire learning-to-learn skills

to learn how to gather, analyze, and report information

to stimulate the pursuit of personal interests

to encourage in-depth understanding of some content areas

The Basics of Independent Study

A successful independent study program is dependent on recognizing and planning for these basic elements:

student self-selection of what is to be studied

cooperative teacher-student planning of what will be studied and how it will be shown

alternative ideas for gathering and processing information

multiple resources which are readily available

teacher intervention through formal and informal student-teacher dialogues

skills integrated with the content area being studied

time specifically allowed for working and conferencing

working and storage space

sharing, feedback, and evaluation opportunities

student recognition for "expertise" and finished project

DEVELOPING AN INDEPENDENT STUDY PLAN

Selecting and delimiting a subject or topic

Discussing and brainstorming possible subareas and questions to explore with the chosen subject or topic

Formulating key questions or issues to pursue and answer

Developing a commitment to a plan and a time sequence

Locating and utilizing multiple resources

Creating a product from the material learned

Sharing with classmates the findings from the study

Evaluating the process and the products from the study and the use of time

Exploring possibilities which could extend the study into new areas of learning

Determining Topics for Independent Study

The selection of topics for students to study can be made from the following variety of sources:

a part of the regular curriculum: an independent study of covered wagons as part of the regular curriculum's social studies unit "The Westward Movement"

an extension of the regular curriculum: an independent study of how cities are developed *after* a study of the Industrial Revolution in the regular curriculum

a personal interest: an independent study related to a hobby, vacation, book read, or item brought in for sharing that a child describes or suggests

a skill to be developed: an independent study related to satisfying an expressed need, such as learning how to weave

a problem to be solved: an independent study focused on resolving a student-centered or real-world problem, such as finding out the causes of inflation

an event or thing observed in the environment: an independent study stimulated by a real or local happening, such as the renovation of a recreational area at the neighborhood park

Identifying the Skills for Independent Study

A successful independent study experience necessitates the *application* of previously acquired skills and the *acquisition* of new skills. Previously acquired skills serve as prerequisites that determine a student's readiness for independent study. New skills are those skills that can be taught to the student as the need for them is identified by the student engaged in the independent study. An assessment tool can be developed and used by the teacher to determine each student's readiness to begin an independent study and to identify the teaching-learning needs before and during the independent-study experience.

TEACHER INTERVENTION

Why the Teacher Intervenes

Student-teacher interaction is necessary during independent study. The interaction may be a formally structured conference or a casual conversation as the teacher circulates around the room while the students are working. The teacher intervenes with the student in order to:

keep in touch

help with problem-solving

provide direction

open up new areas for exploration and production

give encouragement

introduce, teach, and/or reinforce a needed skill

Some Questions to Be Asked when Intervening

Do you have enough materials?

What do you need?

Are you having trouble finding information?

Do you need help in reading any of the material?

Do you understand the information?

Can you find the information you need in order to answer your question(s)?

How much longer do you think it will take to finish this part of the study?

INDEPENDENT STUDY GUIDES

DIRECTION is offered to the student through the use of independent study guides. The guides serve as learning road maps to direct the student through the thinking and action steps of independent study.

ACTIVITIES in the independent study guides provide a range and variety of ways for the student to define a topic, gather and analyze information, and present findings. These activities have been designed to develop the skills of research, the process of problem solving and critical thinking, and the creative expression of findings. In addition, these activities promote skills and attitudes for becoming a self-directed learner.

CREATIVITY is stimulated through activities which stress original methods for gathering, analyzing, and expressing information. High priority is placed on introducing students to learning experiences that extend beyond the usual type of oral and written reports and emphasize *doing* as a vehicle for gathering and assimilating information.

DECISION MAKING is emphasized in the independent study guides by requiring the students to make a choice about which information is to be included in each activity and how the activity is to be produced.

VARIETY is provided for the students through the use of guides that highlight different activities and procedures for conducting an independent study. Some independent study guides direct students toward all the basic steps in conducting an independent study. Others direct students toward specific aspects of an independent study, such as the development of products or the skills of research. The student and the teacher must make a judgment concerning the appropriateness of the independent study guide for each student or the class.

Name _____ Date _____

INDEPENDENT STUDY ASSESSMENT AND PLANNING GUIDE

Directions: Fill in additional prerequisite skills for each step in an independent study. Indicate the student's status for each skill. Use this information to define teaching/learning needs.

Steps in an Independent Study	Prerequisite Skills	Has Mastered	Needs Practice	Has Learned	Teaching/ Learning Needs
Selecting a Topic	Awareness of own interests				
Defining a Problem To Study	Formulating questions Identifying major issues within a topic				
Gathering Information	Using the card catalog Using the encyclopedia. Note-taking				
Analyzing Information	Organizing notes Writing summaries				
Presenting Information	Using materials				

Independent Study Gameboard

This independent study guide gives children alternative suggestions for each step in the independent study process. Each "player" labels a flag with her name and topic of study and rolls the die to move her flag marker through the gameboard. Each step describes a task for players to perform. Children leave their flag, complete the task, return to the gameboard, and continue traveling through the game's path. The gameboard can be placed on a bulletin board or it can be displayed on a table.

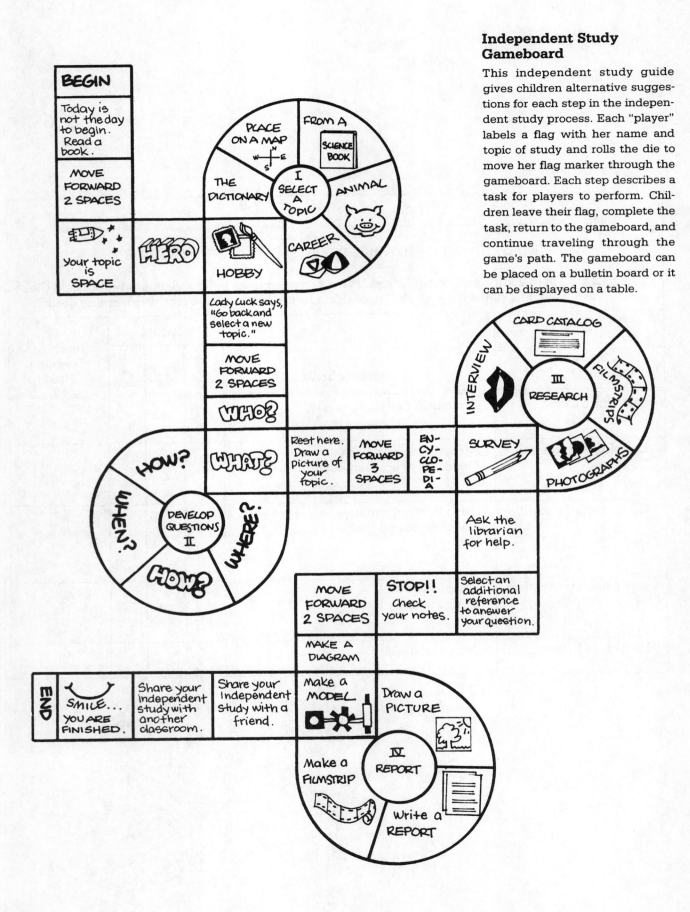

Tic Tac Toe

Students may tic, tac, toe in any direction doing these activities for their independent study.

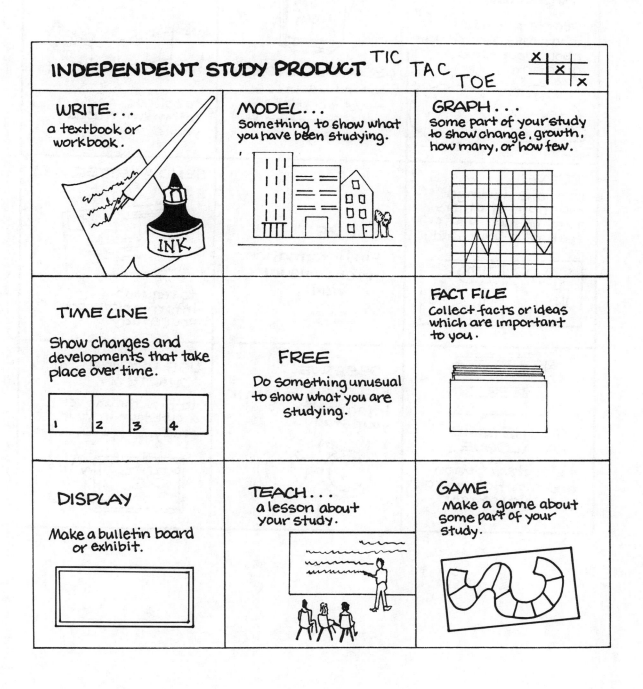

INDEPENDENT STUDY PRODUCT TIC TAC TOE

WRITE...
a textbook or workbook.

MODEL...
Something to show what you have been studying.

GRAPH...
Some part of your study to show change, growth, how many, or how few.

TIME LINE
Show changes and developments that take place over time.

1 2 3 4

FREE
Do something unusual to show what you are studying.

FACT FILE
Collect facts or ideas which are important to you.

DISPLAY
Make a bulletin board or exhibit.

TEACH...
a lesson about your study.

GAME
Make a game about some part of your study.

INDEPENDENT STUDY RESEARCH TIC TAC TOE

INTERVIEW... people to find out what they can tell you about your topic or question.	**USE A DIRECTORY...** to find 3 sources to visit or phone to get information for your study.	**VIEW A FILMSTRIP...** to collect information about your study.
SURVEY... opinions, feelings, reactions of others to some fact, idea, or feature of your study.	**FREE** Find information in an unusual way.	**SEND A LETTER...** to request information about your study.
USE THE CARD CATALOGUE... to locate a fiction and non-fiction book about your study.	**OBSERVE...** Something to gather information about your study.	**USE PICTURES AND CHARTS...** to find the answer to a question in your study.

Independent Study Worksheet

This independent study guide provides children with clues for conducting and recording the progress of their independent study. When completed, the worksheet can be used for the purposes of summarizing findings into a product and evaluating the success of the children's independent study.

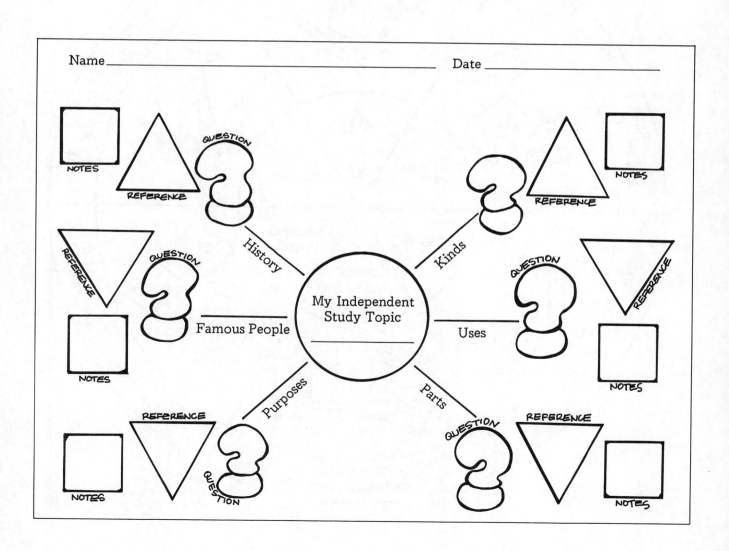

Independent Study Wheel

This chart is to be used by students with a self-selected topic. Students are instructed to go through each type of activity around the wheel. Using the wheel allows children to explore different types of activities and levels of thinking. The outer rim provides students with key words that can be used to develop a task for each step of the wheel.

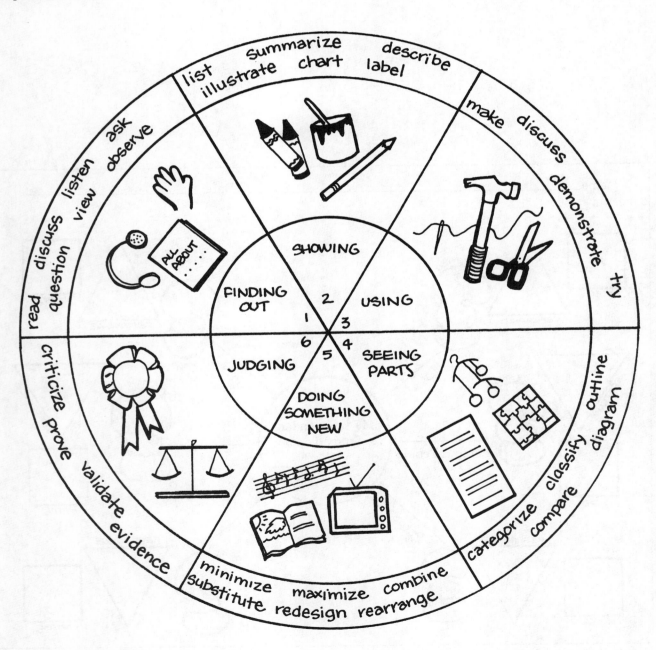

Independent Study Hopscotch

These open-ended activities may be applied to any subject area being studied. The purpose of these activities is to provide new and unusual ways for children to process information. The Hopscotch may be used in numbered sequence or it may be played as a hopscotch game.

WRITE A REVIEW CRITICIZING SOMETHING FROM YOUR STUDY. **6**

MAKE A DIAGRAM TO SHOW THE PART/WHOLE RELATIONSHIP OF SOMETHING IN YOUR STUDY. **4**

WRITE A PLAY TO DRAMATIZE SOMETHING IN YOUR STUDY. **5**

MAKE UP PROBLEMS AND ANSWERS FROM YOUR STUDY. **3**

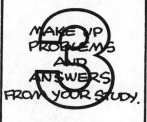

WRITE A TEXTBOOK IN YOUR OWN WORDS ABOUT SOME PART OF YOUR STUDY. **2**

MAKE A DICTIONARY OF IMPORTANT WORDS FOUND IN YOUR STUDY. **1**

Project Alternatives

This independent study guide allows students to make decisions about the type of skill they want to perform and the type of products they want to make. The students match the verbs and the products they have chosen in order to create an independent study activity.

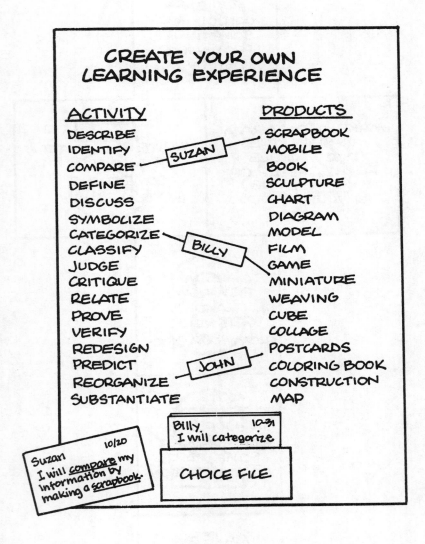

Webbing

Webbing is the process of determining all the possible directions and activities students can explore as a result of their interest in a specific topic or object. This technique, which expands the teacher's and student's awareness for relating and integrating learnings in a given topic, has been developed and used with great success in the British primary schools.

Through webbing, the teacher develops abilities to intervene with the student's learning by asking appropriate questions that stimulate the student to move beyond a narrow consideration of the subject.

The real value of a web is to expand the teacher's thinking about a subject so that there can be spontaneous teacher-student interaction. There is no need to continuously refer to the web, and once the web has been constructed, the teacher can begin to think divergently about subjects and need not go through the formal process with each new topic that is explored in the classroom. Children can be taught to construct their own webs once they understand the intent of the process.

This example is a web a teacher might make when she places magnets in the classroom for children to explore.

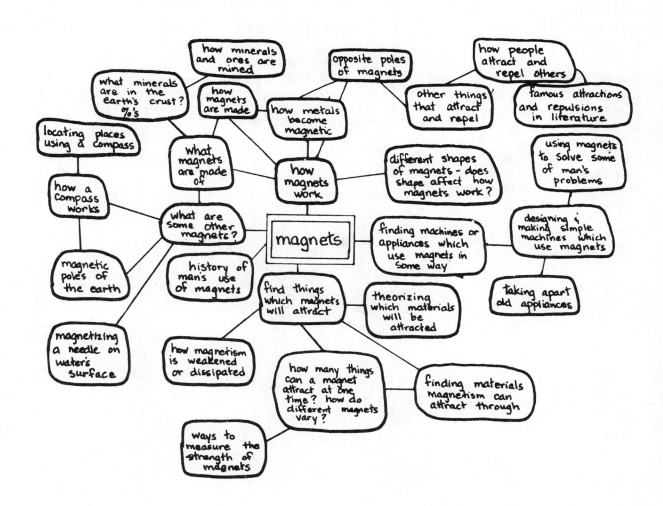

DEVELOPING RESEARCH SKILLS

The teacher can direct the students to charts and worksheets that provide a structure for collecting information. Basically, these activities give students a framework for developing and practicing research skills. The major emphasis for these activities is to assist students in learning how to use references and to *produce* or summarize rather than simply to *reproduce* information. Independent study should be the vehicle for helping students become independent thinkers rather than expert copiers.

Getting My Information

As data is found, it is placed in the appropriate resource pocket in the chart. Students can sort, outline, and compare the type and content of the information they have found.

Resource Key Chain

Keys placed on the key chain can be color-coded in order to show the source from which the key idea was taken. For example, red keys could indicate the key ideas taken from observation as a resource, and blue keys could indicate books used as resources.

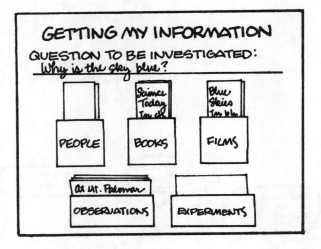

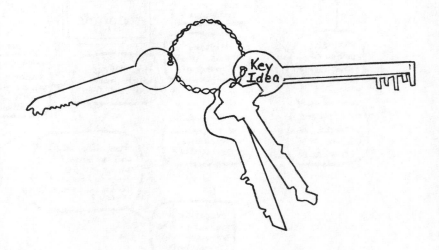

Library Treasure Hunt

This chart can be used to help children gather information from many different types of resources. After children select a topic and formulate a question or identify a problem to investigate, the chart is introduced to the children and is used as a reference for their research activities.

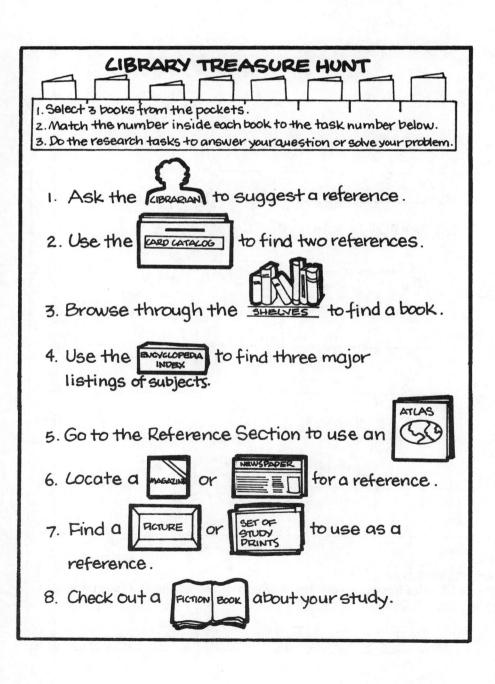

Note-taking Worksheets

The ability to take notes is dependent on an understanding of what should be recorded and how it can be recorded and referenced. The note-taking worksheets reinforce these skills. They can be presented to children in a teacher-directed lesson prior to the initiation of the independent study experience or they can be introduced to children as they have specific needs for notetaking skills while they are engaged in their independent study.

Name_____ Date_____

DON'T PARROT . . . PARAPHRASE

Topic:_____

Question	Direct Quotes	In Your Own Words	Sources: Title Author Publisher Copyright Page Numbers

1. Write your study topic.
2. List the questions you want to investigate.
3. Collect quotes or paraphrase (rewrite in your own words) what you've read in the references.
4. Write your notes under the proper column.
5. List your sources.

Organizing and Summarizing Information Worksheets

Information is gathered to be used in some way. The usability of information is often dependent on knowing how to organize, classify, or categorize data that has been collected. These worksheets provide directed practice in organizing information related to a question under study.

Name _____   Date _____

Legend	Brēf Frms. Tīm Sāvrs

Topic _____

1. Create a legend using symbols to represent the most important words in your study.
2. List the questions you want to research.
3. Take notes on your research. Be sure to use your symbols to save time and energy while note taking.

Question: _____	Question: _____	Question: _____
Notes	Notes	Notes

Name _____ Date _____

NOTABLE-TO-NOT-SO NOTABLE NOTES

Question Under Study _____

1. Identify a question to research and write it in the blank.
2. Use the blocks to write your notes.
3. Cut the note-blocks out on the dotted line.
4. Use the ladder to sort the note-blocks from most important to least important.
5. Write a paragraph based on your notes to answer your question.

Most Important

Least Important

Summary Response
To Question Under Study

Name _____ Date _____

GETTING IT TOGETHER

Question Under Investigation

_____

1. Write your research notes to answer the question.
2. Name two major categories related to your information.
3. Organize your notes into these categories.

NOTES

Title of the Category
_____

1.
2.
3.
4.
5.

Title of the Category
_____

1.
2.
3.
4.
5.

INDEPENDENT STUDY STARTERS

These organizers provide the initial means by which students can:

collect information

record information

share information

develop an idea for an independent study project

Their main function is to give some structured guidelines within which students can work independently. Students complete the basic model, filling it in with their own subject-related information. Words, phrases, sentences, and pictures can be used to record information.

Independent study starters can be made into charts or worksheets. The charts can be hung on a rack or placed on a bulletin board to be made readily accessible to students. Students can copy charts they select; copies of the same chart can be prepared for children to complete. If made into worksheets, the independent study starters can be filed in a box under a title that relates to the skill they reinforce. In either case, the independent study starters can be assigned to students based on diagnosed learning needs or they can be selected by students according to their own independent study needs.

TOPIC: ___Boats___   Meg R.

TYPES	USES
tugs	pull other boats
yachts	personal pleasure trips

TOPIC: _____

TYPES	USES

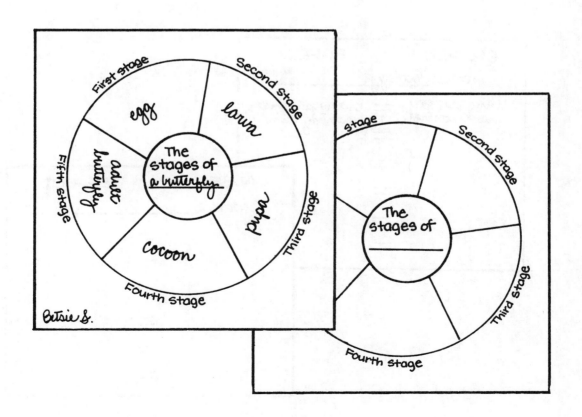

Betsie S.

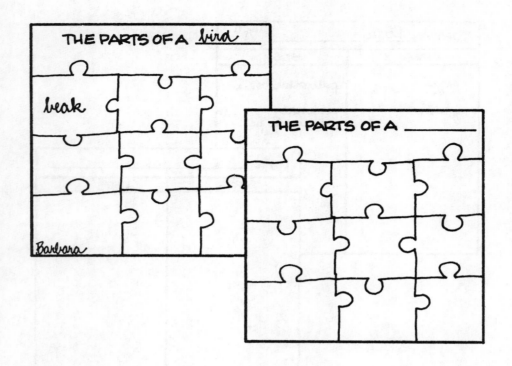

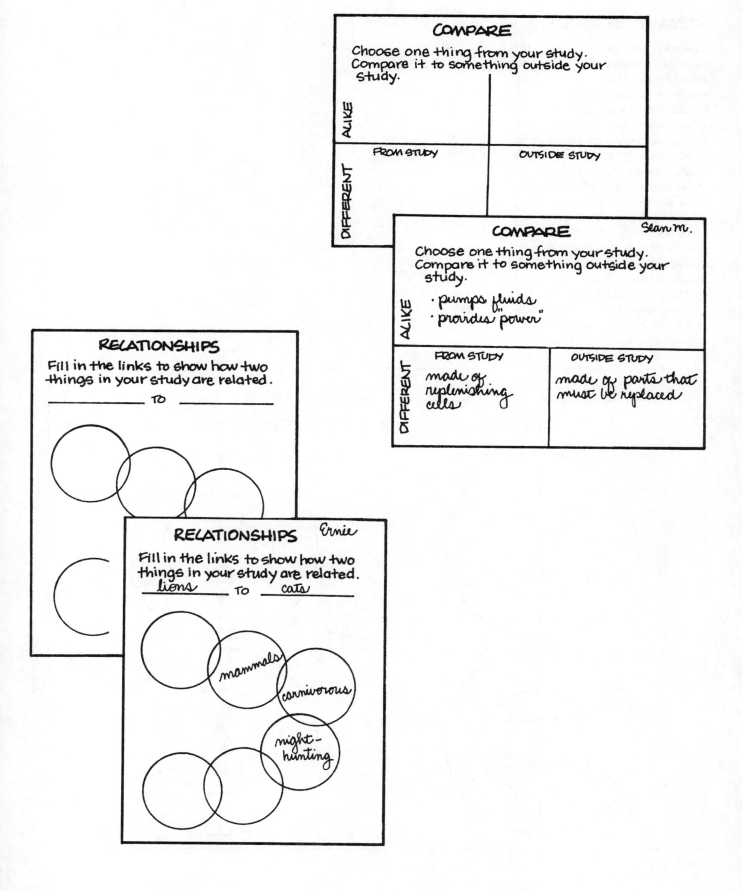

COMPARE

Choose one thing from your study. Compare it to something outside your study.

ALIKE

FROM STUDY	OUTSIDE STUDY

DIFFERENT

COMPARE   Sean M.

Choose one thing from your study. Compare it to something outside your study.

ALIKE
- pumps fluids
- provides "power"

DIFFERENT

FROM STUDY	OUTSIDE STUDY
made of replenishing cells	made of parts that must be replaced

RELATIONSHIPS

Fill in the links to show how two things in your study are related.

_____ TO _____

RELATIONSHIPS   Ernie

Fill in the links to show how two things in your study are related.

lions TO cats

mammals

carnivorous

night-hunting

COMMITTEE STUDY

Independent study does not necessarily mean that a student must work alone. Committee study is an independent study conducted by a group of students who collaborate on tasks. The group determines the activities for each phase of the independent study process and designs procedures for sharing or for dividing up roles and responsibilities needed to execute the task. Children can form their own Committee Study groups based on shared interests, friendship, like abilities, or needs. Teachers can also assign students to Committee Study groups. The teacher needs to prepare students, through lessons or discussion groups, for the problems that

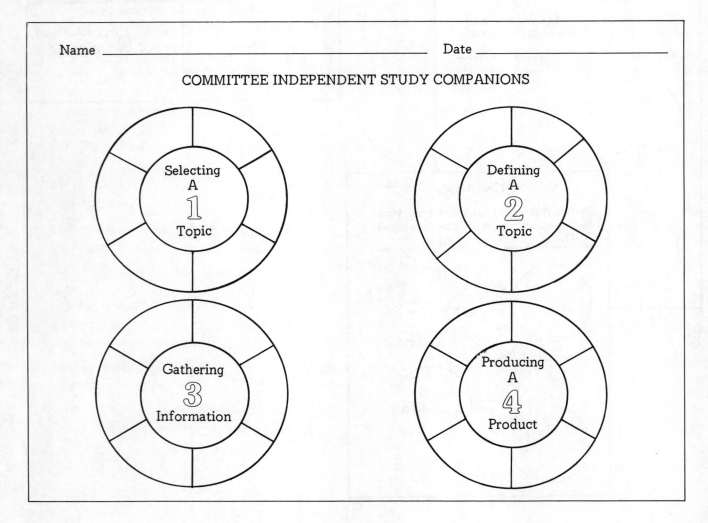

Name _____ Date _____

COMMITTEE INDEPENDENT STUDY COMPANIONS

Selecting
A
1
Topic

Defining
A
2
Topic

Gathering
3
Information

Producing
A
4
Product

can arise from group work and help them develop possible solutions for these problems. Learning to work in a group and developing an understanding and appreciation for group dynamics are important outcomes of committee independent study.

These worksheets outline the four basic steps in a Committee Study. Working as a group, the children identify specific tasks for each group member to do for each step of the independent study. Children color in their assigned task after it is completed. Each colored wheel indicates the cooperative efforts of the group toward the independent study experience.

Name_____ Date_____

COMMITTEE STUDY

Directions: 1. Determine the tasks for each step of your independent study.
2. Fill in the worksheet to show which tasks will be done by the total group and which tasks will be done by individual members of the group.

TOGETHER	S P E of T Independent S Study	ALONE
We'll _____	1. Select a Topic	I'll _____ I'll _____ I'll _____ I'll _____
We'll _____	2. Define the Problem	I'll _____ I'll _____ I'll _____ I'll _____
We'll _____	3. Research	I'll _____ I'll _____ I'll _____ I'll _____
We'll _____	4. Report	I'll _____ I'll _____ I'll _____ I'll _____

SHARING INDEPENDENT STUDY PRODUCTS

How the information is converted into an independent study product is dependent on the student's artistic interests, the alternatives the teacher has presented, and the availability of raw materials. Creative independent study products result when students are allowed to select and manipulate raw materials. Collecting and placing raw materials in a specific location within the room acts as a stimulus for possible independent study products. Students should be encouraged to mix and match materials and use the materials in new and different ways.

Products provide a means for presenting the learnings of an independent study, giving recognition to the students' accomplishments and stimulating independent study possibilities for other children. These products can be placed in the environment or they can be shared orally with other students.

Project Cubes

Project cubes are a method of sharing information and a way to motivate others toward independent study.

Boxes of all shapes and sizes can be used to show the parts of a particular study.

Within one box the student can depict on six sides: subtopics, answers to questions, or concepts learned. With many boxes the student can build a pyramid to illustrate the varying aspects of his study.

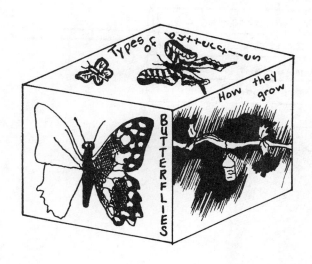

Mobile

Some aspect or concept of the student's independent study can be creatively structured into a mobile art form.

Venetian Blinds and Window Shades

Information from the student's independent study can be exhibited on venetian blinds and window shades. They can be used for time lines, flow charts, and murals. They are easily stored and displayed.

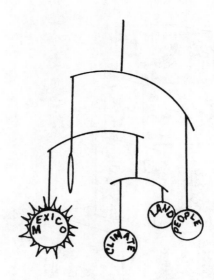

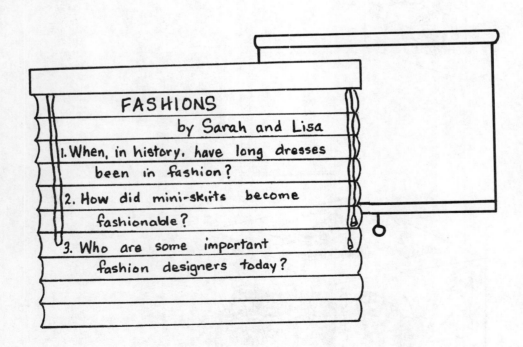

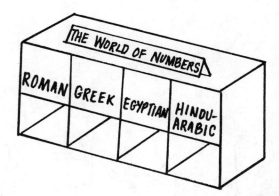

Museum

Formed from a box, the museum houses the personal treasures the student has collected or made in relationship to the topic he has studied.

Cans

Each can indicates a sub-area, question, or phase of the student's independent study and becomes a compartment for facts, pictures, and items within that category.

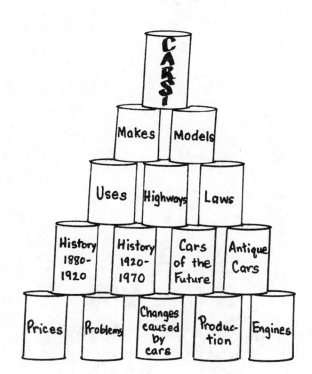

STORING PROJECTS

While students engage in independent study, the amount and types of products in progress can become cumbersome. Storage containers can be created which save space while still making the projects accessible.

Sacks

A collection of all types of shopping bags can become storage containers. Hung on hooks, knobs, backs of chairs, coat racks, or hangers, these receptacles are transportable and conveniently kept so that students can easily store their independent study materials.

Ice Cream Containers

Five-gallon ice cream containers can be used to store independent study projects. These containers can be stacked to form a set of cubicles by punching holes through them and then securing them with string, yarn, or wire. They can also be stacked separately so that children can pick them up and take them to the area where they will work. Materials needed for the study (books, notes, paper, etc.), as well as the project in progress, can be kept within the container.

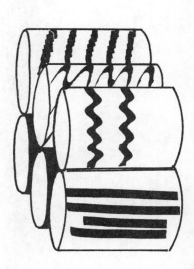

~CONTRACT~

_____ with _____
(student)   (teacher)

SUBJECT: _____

<u>CONTRACTUAL CONDITIONS</u>

What I want to find out:	How I will show what I learned:
_____	_____
_____	_____
_____	_____
_____	_____

DUE DATE: _____
CONSEQUENCES: _____

NAME: _____ DUE DATE: _____

Planning Date: _____

Subject of my study: _____

What I want to find out: _____
_____
_____

Evaluation: _____
_____

Signed: _____   _____
        (student)   (teacher)

RECORD KEEPING

The purpose of independent study record-keeping devices is to encourage student responsibility while keeping the teacher apprised of what the student has been doing.

Contract

Contracts such as these provide a teacher-student agreement within a given time limit.

The expectations for the study are clearly defined by the student with the assistance of the teacher. The contract represents a commitment for a course of action.

Log

This log assists the student in planning and following through on his or her independent study. It also may serve to help the student evaluate his or her progress.

KEEPING TRACK
OF MY
INDEPENDENT
STUDY

LOG OF MY INDEPENDENT STUDY			
Date	Accomplishments	Evaluation	Next step (Plans)

Individual Thermometer

Each student records the progress of his independent study as he moves through the various activities listed on the thermometer.

Group Thermometer

The five thermometers on the bulletin board indicate major activities each student is expected to complete. As a student finishes the activity, she computes the class percentage on the corresponding thermometer.

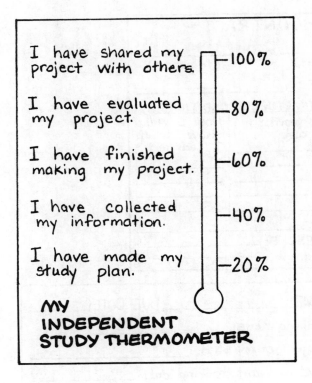

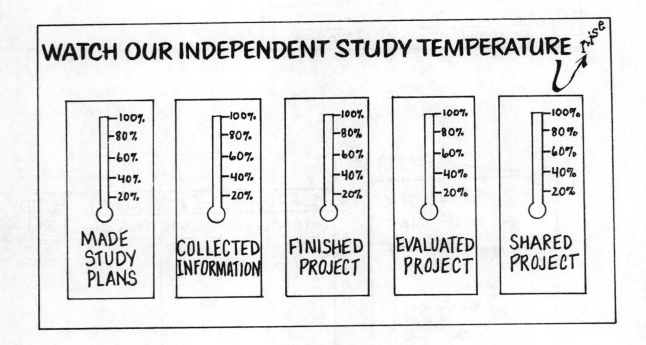

Group Ladder

Each rung of the ladder indicates an activity the learner must do in sequence as part of the independent study program. Students move their markers as they complete each step of the independent study program.

Individual Ladder

One bulletin board can be set aside for independent study record keeping. Each student's ladder represents an outline of the student's study plan as well as her progress in completing the plan.

EVALUATION

Key Questions the Teacher Might Discuss with the Student During an Evaluation

What do you like best about the project you are doing (or have completed)? Why?

What parts of your project caused you difficulties? How did you solve these problems?

What new skills did you learn while working on the project (such as typing, lettering, outlining, etc.)?

What sources of information did you use? Did all the sources agree?

Was your independent study plan reasonable as far as goals and time allotment were concerned? How might your plan have been changed?

How could other students use your project?

How did you collect or keep track of your information while you were studying? Can you think of another method to use?

What new ideas for another study did you get from the one you have just finished?

Do you have any unanswered questions about your subject? How might you find the answers?

How could you challenge or interest others to study your subject?

Student Self-Evaluation

This is a self-administered, subjective evaluation. The instrument for this evaluation is developed by the teacher and the student in relationship to the goals of the independent study plan.

Class Sharing

The student is given an opportunity to orally present the end-product of his independent study to the class. Class members respond with questions and comments that may clarify or challenge the student's learnings. "The Key Questions the Teacher Might Discuss with the Student," as listed under *Teacher-Student Conferences*, might also be used in this situation. The group should develop standards that serve as a reference as they share and discuss their independent studies.

Independent Study Evaluation Committee

This committee is made up of from six to eight classmates chosen by the students and the teacher. The standards for evaluation and discussion of the student's independent study are developed by the group. The evaluation of the independent study is a composite of the group's reaction to it. Some sample questions the committee might direct to the student include:

Did the student try to use many sources for his information?

Did she conference with the teacher when she needed help?

Did she try to share her information in new and unusual ways?

Was he able to summarize what he learned?

Example: Independent Study Profile

Name _____ Subject _____ Date _____

Directions: Place a check on each continuum to show how you feel about the independent study you have completed.

1. Use of Resources
   many _____ few
   same _____ different

2. Finished Project (or Product)
   ordinary _____ unlike any others
   written _____ constructed

3. Use of Time
   wasted _____ worked hard

4. Feelings About the Study
   satisfied _____ dissatisfied
   learned enough _____ need to learn more

Name_____ Date_____

HOW DOES YOUR GARDEN GROW?

Draw different petals around each flower. Cut and paste the flowers to the stems in ABC order.

R

M

G

D

A

O

How many words can you make using the letters in your flower pot?

Y

P

S

E

Name —————

Date —————

WASH DAY ALPHABETIZING

Cut and paste the words on each piece of clothing in alphabetical order.

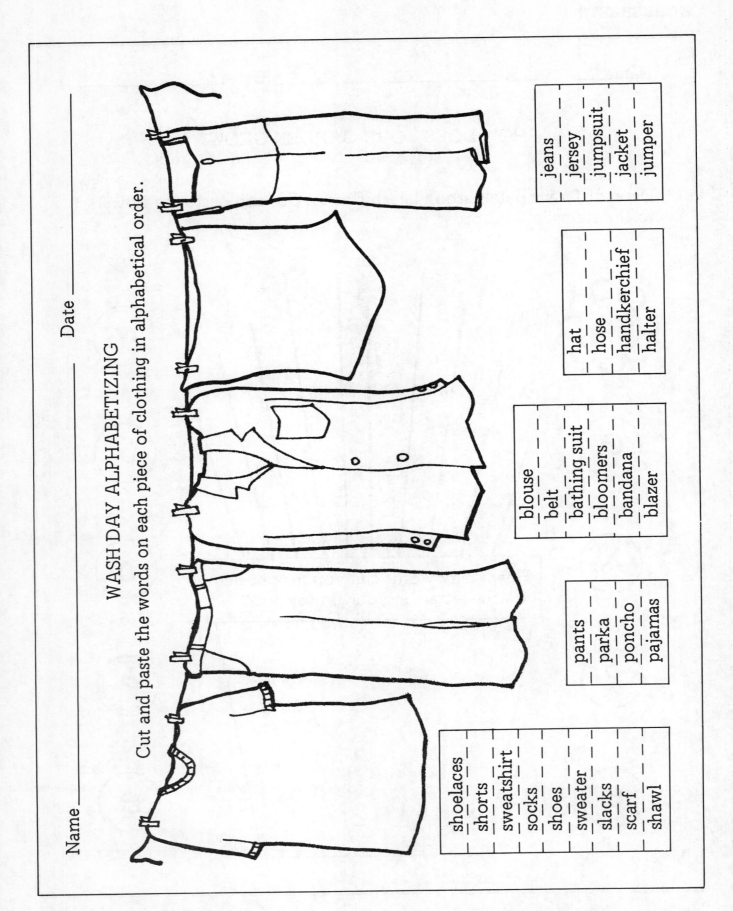

jeans
jersey
jumpsuit
jacket
jumper

hat
hose
handkerchief
halter

blouse
belt
bathing suit
bloomers
bandana
blazer

pants
parka
poncho
pajamas

shoelaces
shorts
sweatshirt
socks
shoes
sweater
slacks
scarf
shawl

Name —————

Date —————

Observe and study the buildings in your neighborhood or city. Complete the form below for buildings in each category.

	Date Built	Where Located	Bldg. Use Originally & Present	Outstanding Features	Architect	Materials	Design Appropriate to Surroundings	Rating	Recommendations
School									
Place of Worship									
Recreation									
Government									
Store									
Home									

Name_____ Date_____

Prepare a multiple choice test for a classmate to take. Questions might pertain to architecture vocabulary, famous architects, architect's tools, or a math problem to solve.

If the test taker successfully completes your test, present him with an Architect Tech diploma.

ARCHITECT'S TECH TEST

	A	B	C	D
1.	☐	☐	☐	☐
2.	☐	☐	☐	☐
3.	☐	☐	☐	☐
4.	☐	☐	☐	☐
5.	☐	☐	☐	☐
6.	☐	☐	☐	☐
7.	☐	☐	☐	☐
8.	☐	☐	☐	☐

- -

ARCHITECT'S TECH DIPLOMA

Having successfully completed the test designed by

_____
test maker

_____
test taker

is awarded this diploma on _____.
date

This is one of my favorite works because:

Interesting notes about the work or artist:
Country work was executed in:
Date of work:
Medium:
Artist:
Title of work:

Name _____ Date _____

This is one of my favorite works because:

Interesting notes about the work or artist:
Country work was executed in:
Date of work:
Medium:
Artist:
Title of work:

Name _____ Date _____

Name_____ Date_____

Title of work:_____
Artist:_____
Medium:_____
Date of work:_____
Country work was executed in:_____
Interesting notes about the work or artist:_____

This is one of my favorite works because:_____

A Guide to

_____'s

Favorite Works

of Art

Name _____ Date _____

Write a Critic's Corner column that compares two works of art. In making your comparison think about artist's style, reason for work, medium used, when created, subject matter, mood of work and use of elements of art.

Critic's Corner

Title of work _____   DIFFERENCES _____

Artist _____   _____

Medium _____   _____

Date of Work _____   _____

Title of work _____   _____

Artist _____   _____

Medium _____   _____

Date of Work _____   _____

SIMILARITIES _____   SUMMARY _____

_____   _____

_____   _____

_____   _____

_____   _____

_____   _____

_____   _____

_____   _____

_____   _____

Name _____

Date _____

OH SAY, CAN YOU SEE?

Choose a work of art and find out what people see in it. Take along a picture of the work you have chosen.

Title of work: _____

Artist's Name: _____

Interview these people. Write their names in the spaces.	Ask them these questions. "What do you think this work is about?" "What things or emotions do you see in the work?"	Do they like the work?		How much would they pay for it?
		Yes	No	
Someone under six years of age				
Someone your age				
A teenager				
Someone with glasses				
Someone with a mustache				
Someone who "towers" above you				
Someone wearing your favorite color				

(See page 46) ART APPRECIATION / **WS-7**

Name _____ Date _____

Language _____

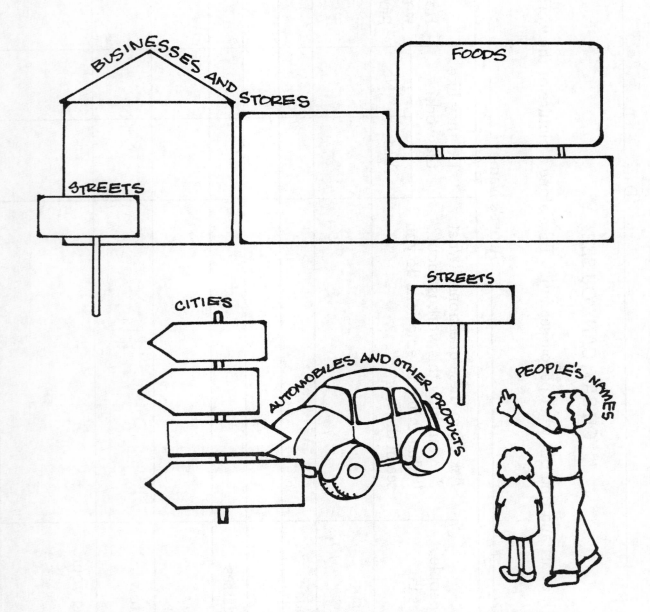

Complete the picture by writing in names of streets, cities, auto-mobiles, people, food, and businesses in your city that come from the language you are studying. If you can't find enough words in your city, write in foreign words of your choosing (in the same language, of course). You may add other objects to the picture.

FOREIGN FUNNIES

Finish each panel of the cartoon strip by drawing a setting or background, objects, animals or other people. Write dialogue for the cartoon in the language you are studying.

(See page 51) BILINGUAL / **WS-9**

Name ———————————————— Date ——————————

 CAN YOU BUDGET?

You get $10 allowance a month (4 weeks). You must buy lunch at school two times a week. Lunch costs 50¢. You also have to buy your school supplies. You may spend or save any money that is left.

Total $10 a month

Lunch   50¢ a time

               = ——————— two times a week

               = ——————— 4 weeks

Total lunch cost   ———————

Money left after lunches   ———————

School supplies for the month $2

Money left after expenses   ———————

If you budget your money, how much extra will
you have to spend or save each week?   ———————

How much each school day?   ———————

How will you spend it? ————————————————————————————

Where will you spend it? ———————————————————————————

——

——

PRICE PER MEASURE

Which do you think is the better buy? Figure out the price per measure to be sure.

	Check the one you think will be the better buy	Figure out and write in each products PPM
Clean-All Detergent 15 oz. box $1.50	☐	_____
Clean-All Giant Economy Size 30 oz. $3.00	☐	_____
Orange-O Orange Juice Concentrate 12 oz. makes ½ gallon $1.28	☐	_____
Fresh orange juice 1 quart $.96	☐	_____
Delicious Whole Wheat Bread 1 lb. loaf $1.12	☐	_____
Scrumptious Whole Wheat Bread 12 oz. Loaf $.96	☐	_____
See Through Window Cleaner 20 oz. bottle $1.00	☐	_____
See Through Trial Size 5 oz. bottle $.35	☐	_____
Moca-Coca 2 litre bottle $.75	☐	_____
Moca-Coca 6-pack (354 ml. per can) $1.50	☐	_____

Name _____ Date _____

Sometimes recipes make more or less than you need. These recipes have to be changed to make the right amount for you.

Double this recipe of trail mix.

TRAIL MIX

150 g. nuts   _____ g.
150 g. raisins   _____ g.
100 g. sunflower seeds   _____ g.
125 g. carob chips   _____ g.

Halve this recipe for fruit salad.

FRUIT SALAD

700 g. grapes   _____ g.
500 g. pineapple   _____ g.
200 g. strawberries   _____ g.
400 g. bananas   _____ g.
Top with 300 g. yogurt   _____ g.

Triple this recipe for yourself and eight friends to enjoy.

BANANA NOG

480 ml. cold milk   _____ ml.
  2 eggs   _____ eggs
 15 ml. honey   _____ ml.
  5 ml. vanilla   _____ ml.
  1 large banana   _____ bananas
Blend well.

Name_____ Date_____

DO YOU KNOW BASIC INGREDIENTS?

If you use the wrong kind of sugar, you might have gritty frosting.
If you use the wrong kind of flour, your cake might feel like a
rock. If you use a different kind of oil than your recipe calls for,
your pancakes might taste like olives. Better find out the differences!

Kinds of Sugar   Description

_____   _____
_____   _____
_____   _____
_____   _____

Which is the best for you?_____ The worst?_____
Why?_____

Kinds of Flour   Description

_____   _____
_____   _____
_____   _____
_____   _____

Which is the best for you?_____ The worst?_____
Why?_____

Kinds of Oil   Description

_____   _____
_____   _____
_____   _____
_____   _____

Which is the best for you?_____ The worst?_____
Why?_____

Now write which kind of each ingredient would be best.

_____sugar for frosting _____flour for cakes

olive oil is good for _____

Name_____ Date_____

DOT – TO – DOT MONSTER CUT

Cut these lines between the numbers to make a monster.

1-2 〜〜〜〜〜
3-4 ————
5-6 ————
7-8 ————
9-10 〜〜〜〜

11-12 〜〜〜〜〜
13-14 〈〈〈〈〈〈〈
15-16 〜〜〜〜〜〜
17-18 ————

DOT – TO – DOT MONSTER CUT

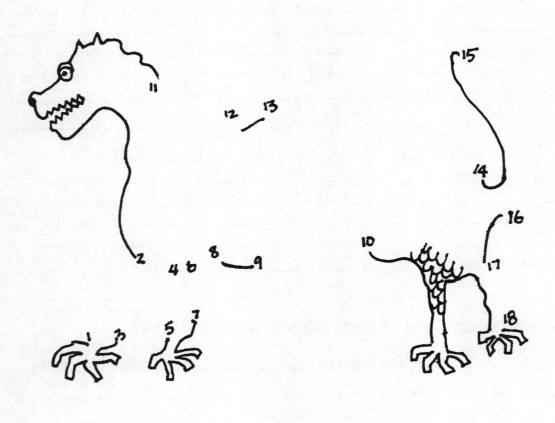

Name _____

Date _____

MAKING FRIENDS

1. FOLD the paper along the dotted lines.
2. CUT out the friends.
3. PASTE clothes on the friends.
4. CUT and PASTE one more friend and add the friend to the group.
5. Use a CRAYON to name all your friends.
6. Write your name on the back. Use a different color for each letter.

1.

2.

Name_____ Date_____

HARD-TO-CUT-OUTS

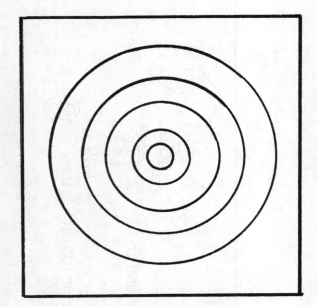

Cut out the third circle.

Cut around the snowflake.

Cut the board out of
man's hand.

Cut the fruit out of
the basket.

Name_____ Date_____

Choose one building to look at. Categorize all of the items at the location (a home, an apartment, a store, a yard, a church) by listing them under the following headings.

Made of Wood

_____
_____
_____
_____

Growing Things

_____
_____
_____
_____

Made of Cement,
Brick, Plaster

_____
_____
_____
_____

Containing or
Made of Glass

_____
_____
_____
_____

Made of Metal

_____
_____
_____
_____

Made of Plastic

_____
_____
_____
_____

Name _____

Date _____

A NEIGHBORHOOD WALK

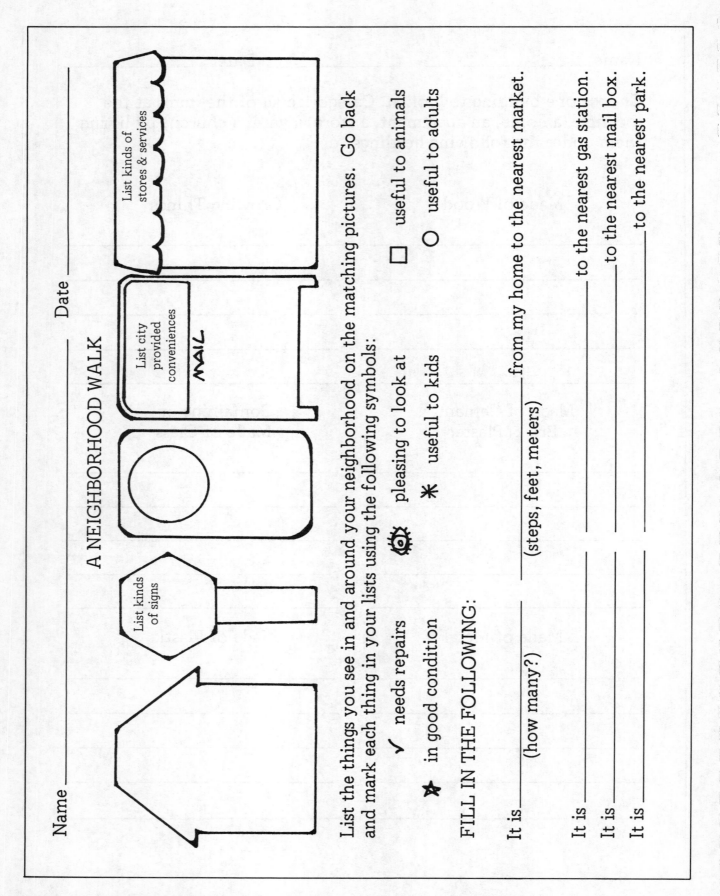

List kinds of signs

List city provided conveniences

MAIL

List kinds of stores & services

List the things you see in and around your neighborhood on the matching pictures. Go back and mark each thing in your lists using the following symbols:

⊙ pleasing to look at

□ useful to animals

✓ needs repairs

✱ useful to kids

○ useful to adults

★ in good condition

FILL IN THE FOLLOWING:

It is _____ _____ from my home to the nearest market.
    (how many?)   (steps, feet, meters)

It is _____ to the nearest gas station.

It is _____ to the nearest mail box.

It is _____ to the nearest park.

Name _____ Date _____

POLLUTION – AN ECOLOGICAL PROBLEM
"Ecology Apologies"

1. Write one cause for each type of pollution.
2. Tell how one thing is affected by each type of pollution.
3. For each kind of pollution, write two "ecology apologies": things people say to try to make up for what we've lost or are losing.

A CAUSE: Nuclear wastes are buried in the ground.

A CAUSE:

AN EFFECT: People exposed to radioactivity have a greater chance of getting cancer.

AN EFFECT:

APOLOGIES:

1. It costs a lot to get rid of wastes. Do you want to pay for it? _____
_____

2. _____
_____

APOLOGIES:

1. _____
_____
_____

2. _____
_____

A CAUSE:

AN EFFECT:

APOLOGIES:

1. _____

2. _____

A CAUSE:

AN EFFECT:

APOLOGIES:

1. _____

2. _____

A CAUSE:

AN EFFECT:

APOLOGIES:

1. _____

2. _____

A CAUSE:

AN EFFECT:

APOLOGIES:

1. _____

2. _____

Name_____ Date_____

ENVIRONMENTAL NUMBER FACTS

<u>POPULATION NUMBER FACTS</u> Show the following facts in graph form.

1. About 74,000,000,000 persons have lived on the earth in the last 600,000 years.

2. The world population in 1970 was about 3,600,000,000. By the year 2000 it will be about 6,500,000,000.

3. The U.S. population in 1776 was about 4,000,000. In 1976, it was about 228,000,000. The U.S. population in 1970 was about 205,000,000. By the year 2040 it will probably double, to about 410,000,000.

<u>PERSONAL and PRODUCTION NUMBER FACTS</u> Chart the following information (except no. 5 and no. 6) in metric measurements.

1. Each person in the U.S. uses almost 60 gallons of water each day.

2. Each person in the U.S. uses almost 19 gallons of water each day for bathing.

3. A U.S. family of four eats about 260 pounds of pork each year.

4. Each Canadian eats about 96 pounds of beef each year.

5. Each American throws away about 5 pounds of rubbish daily.

6. Each car in the U.S. burns about 306 gallons of gas every year.

7. It takes about 17 trees to make 1 ton of newsprint.

8. About 48 acres of land must be cleared to build 1 mile of super-highway.

9. Oil refineries use about 500 gallons of water to produce 1 gallon of gas.

10. Paper companies use about 50 gallons of water to make 1 pound of paperboard.

Name _____ Date _____

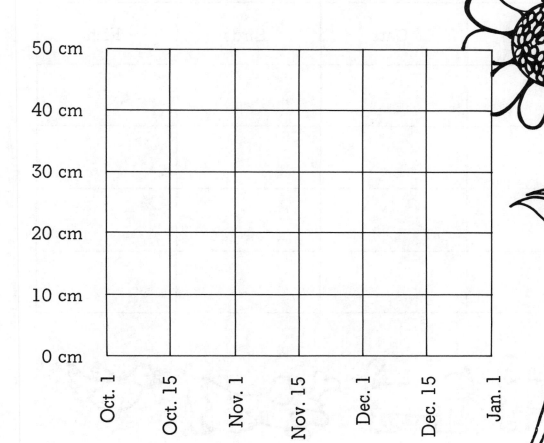

MY SUNFLOWER GROWS UP

	Oct. 1	Oct. 15	Nov. 1	Nov. 15	Dec. 1	Dec. 15	Jan. 1

50 cm
40 cm
30 cm
20 cm
10 cm
0 cm

Make a line graph of this information:

   Oct. 1   —   0 cm
   Oct. 15 —   5 cm
   Nov. 1   — 10 cm
   Nov. 15 — 20 cm
   Dec. 1   — 25 cm
   Dec. 15 — 30 cm
   Jan. 1   — 50 cm

    (See page 80) GRAPHING / **WS-21**

Name _____ Date _____

MY FRIEND'S PETS

Dogs	Cats	Birds	Fish

Cut out these pictures and paste them on the graph.

Name_____ Date _____

FEELING FINE AND OTHERWISE

Make the following observations when you are feeling fine:

Heart: about _____beats per minute

Temperature: about _____

Breathing rate: about _____breaths per minute

Skin color: _____

Other characteristics:

But how about when you feel:

sad

Heart_____

Temperature_____

Breathing_____

Skin_____

Other _____

excited

Heart _____

Temperature_____

Breathing_____

Skin_____

Other _____

nervous

Heart _____

Temperature_____

Breathing_____

Skin_____

Other _____

angry

Heart _____

Temperature_____

Breathing_____

Skin_____

Other _____

Name_____ Date_____

Different sports and physical activities use and strengthen muscles in different parts of the body. First complete the lists below. Then, using these lists, write the type of sport or physical activity on the part of the body that is exercised.

Sports   Other Physical Activities

_____   _____
_____   _____
_____   _____
_____   _____
_____   _____
_____   _____
_____   _____

Name _____

Date _____

HOW MUCH SLEEP DO YOU NEED?

Z-Z-Z-Z-Z-Z-Z-Z-Z-Z-Z

Keep track of the amount of sleep you get every night for one week.
Show the results of this record using any method of graphing you choose.

	Time I went to bed	Time I got up	No. of hours I slept	In the morning I was (check ✓) very rested	a little rested	not rested
Monday	____ pm	____ pm	_____	☐	☐	☐
Tuesday	____ pm	____ pm	_____	☐	☐	☐
Wednesday	____ pm	____ pm	_____	☐	☐	☐
Thursday	____ pm	____ pm	_____	☐	☐	☐
Friday	____ pm	____ pm	_____	☐	☐	☐
Saturday	____ pm	____ pm	_____	☐	☐	☐
Sunday	____ pm	____ pm	_____	☐	☐	☐

From this information I think I need _____ hours of sleep each night.

Name _____ Date _____

Show which parts of a story are believable and which parts are make believe.

State the reasons for your decisions.

Story Title: _____

Believable		Make Believe	
Part	Reasons	Part	Reasons

Name _____ Date _____

Stories often grow out of American history. Research a hero for one of the times on the time line. Use the hero as a character in a mystery, folk tale, or biography.

| 1725 | 1750 | 1775 | 1800 | 1825 | 1850 | 1875 | 1900 | 1925 | 1950 |

Hero: _____

_____

Research Findings: _____

_____

_____

Type of Story: _____

Title of Story: _____

_____

Story: _____

_____

_____

_____

_____

GUESS THE BOOK

1. Use a book you have read with this worksheet.
2. Fill in a different type of clue for the four categories each day.

   Day One — Use a color clue.   Day Four — Use a phrase clue.
   Day Two — Use a symbol clue.   Day Five — Use a sentence clue.
   Day Three — Use a word clue.

3. Display this worksheet for your classmates.
4. Tell your classmates to read the clues to name the book. The first
   person to name the book you are describing wins the Guess the
   Book game.

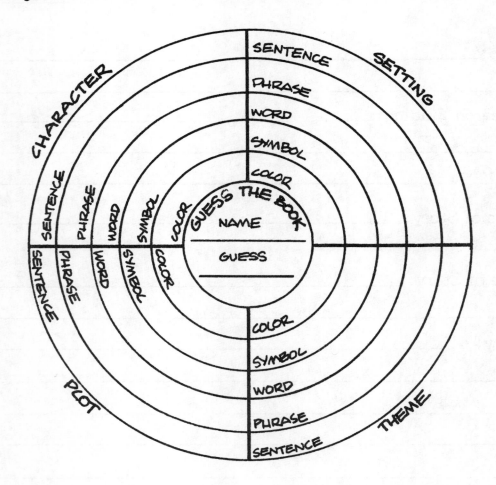

Name _____ Date _____

What kind of map would you use to find out . . .

what to wear to visit a new city		
which bus to take		
location of the park		
how people live there		
which mountains are nearby		
which areas have the most people		

Name _____ Date _____

MAP COLLECTOR CLUB APPLICATION

Name of applicant: _____

Address of applicant: _____

Latitude and longitude of your town: _____

Describe the map you have found to contribute to the club's files:

_____

_____

Tell about your personal interest in maps: _____

_____

Draw a rough outline of your state and show your town's approximate location.

List map activities and skillwork you have completed:

1.

2.

3.

4.

Give this portion of the application to a member of the Map Club, who will then give you 5 questions or tasks related to maps.

Member's name: _____ Applicant's name: _____

Map used: _____

The 5 questions or tasks were: Check if completed satisfactorily:

1.   _____

2.   _____

3.   _____

4.   _____

5.   _____

Date of test: _____

Name _____ Date_____

RAINBOW MEASURING

What will you get when you mix water of various colors together?
Do it and see! Use water with food coloring added to it.

80 ml. red + 40 ml. yellow = _____ ml. _____

20 ml. green + 20 ml. red = _____ml. _____

10 ml. yellow + 10 ml. red + 10 ml. blue = _____ ml._____

Now make up your own. Guess what color you think you will get.

Were you right?

My Rainbow Equations:	My guess of color results:	The actual colors I got:
1. _____	_____	_____
2. _____	_____	_____
3. _____	_____	_____

        (See page 99) MEASUREMENT / **WS-31**

Name_____ Date_____

Gather several containers of different sizes. Estimate how many litres or millilitres each will hold. Use water and a litre measure to check your estimates.

_____ _____   _____ _____
Estimate   Actual   Estimate   Actual

_____ _____   _____ _____
Estimate   Actual   Estimate   Actual

Name _____

Date _____

The same job can often be done both by hand and by machine. Use words or pictures to show the different ways below.

Job to be done	By hand	By machine
mashing a banana		
sanding a tabletop		
beating eggs		

(See page 103) MECHANICAL EXPLORATION / **WS-33**

Name_____ Date_____

MACHINE TAKE-APART

1. Choose an item to take apart.
   Name it._____

   _____

2. Is it electric?_____If yes, does it have an electric motor?_____
   If yes, tell what the motor does. _____

   _____

3. Does it have an electric heating element? _____
   If yes, where is it and what does it heat?_____

   _____

4. If it's not electric, what makes it work?_____

   _____

5. Draw a diagram of how the item works.

1

Career Title: _____

Illustration
(draw or cut out
and paste)

Check any media in which one might find employment:

☐ newspapers ☐ TV-entertainment
☐ news magazines ☐ TV-news, public affairs
☐ topical magazines ☐ radio-entertainment
   name type: _____ ☐ feature films
☐ documentary film
☐ recording industry

List any related fields in which employment may be found:

_____
_____

MEDIA CAREER GUIDE

_____
(career title)

4

RESOURCE LIST to help you learn more about the job

Books:
_____
_____
_____

Films, TV shows, etc.
_____
_____

Companies/People to visit or interview:
_____
_____
_____

Author of article: _____

MEDIA CAREER GUIDE

3

EDUCATION _____

_____

_____

OTHER TRAINING _____

_____

MEDIA CAREER
GUIDE

JOB HIGHLIGHTS — a brief description of activities, pay range, benefits, etc. _____

_____

JOB QUALIFICATIONS — personal qualities, talents, and interests other than education _____

_____

MEDIA CAREER
GUIDE

2

Name _____

Date _____

MEDIA NEWS COVERAGE

1. Choose one story from the TV evening news. Briefly describe it in the DAY 1 box below.

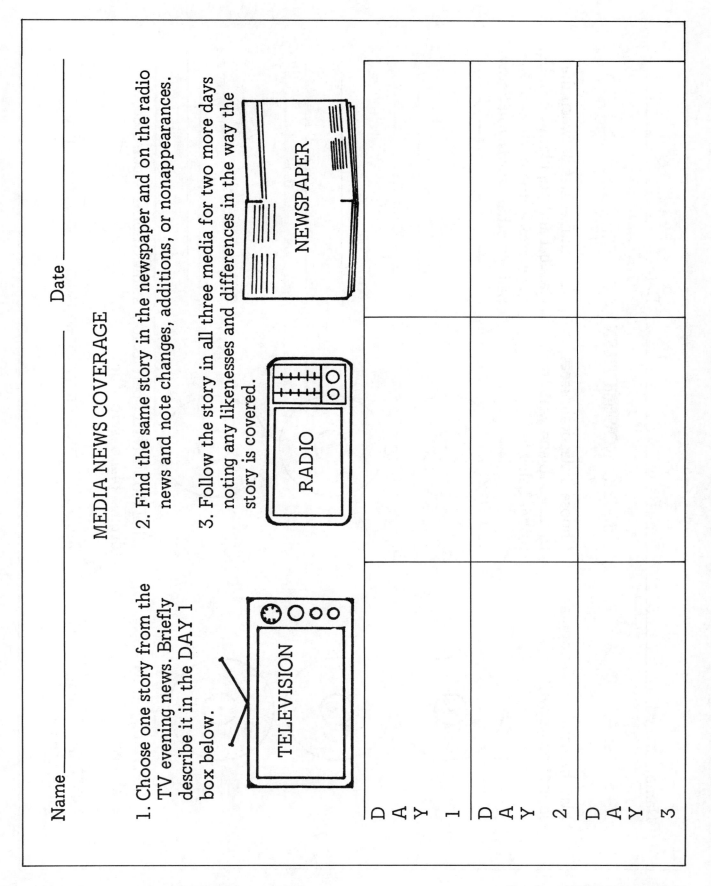

TELEVISION

RADIO

NEWSPAPER

2. Find the same story in the newspaper and on the radio news and note changes, additions, or nonappearances.

3. Follow the story in all three media for two more days noting any likenesses and differences in the way the story is covered.

D A Y 1		
D A Y 2		
D A Y 3		

Name _____

Date _____

MUSIC: NOW and THEN

List the names of 3 popular songs you know.

Choose 3 classical pieces to listen to and write their names below.

Write similarities between the classical and popular pieces. Use the words at the bottom of the page or other words you know.

1. _____
_____

2. _____
_____

3. _____
_____

INSTRUMENTS: percussion strings horns electronic drums piano solo duet

MELODY: smooth sweet-sounding rising and falling

TEMPO: fast slow break-neck

RHYTHM: catchy even smooth hard

_____'S LISTENING RECORD

1. Listen to two selections from each category named on the grooves. On the same groove, write in titles, composers, performers (if possible).

2. Mark each selection with one of these ratings:

   + would like to hear again soon

   o would be OK to hear again someday

   - wouldn't like to hear again

   * would like to hear other things from this category

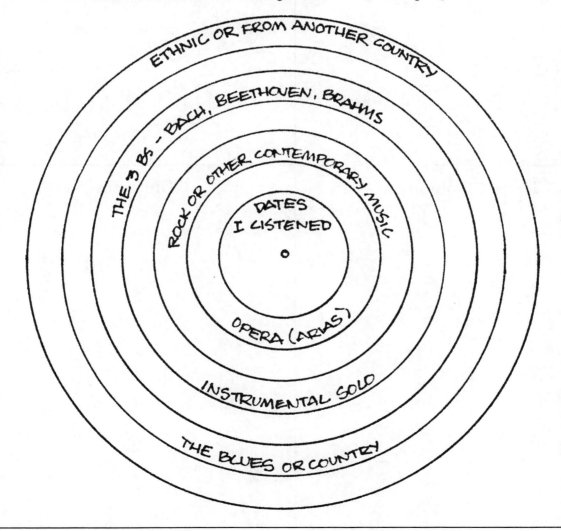

Name_____ Date_____

MATCH

SCIENCE FICTION TO
SCIENCE NONFICTION

Find things in Science Fiction stories which can be put into these
real scientific categories.

Space Vehicles	Natural Phenomena
Tools & Equipment	**Uniforms**

Name_____ Date_____

DO YOU WANT TO BE AN ASTRONAUT?

Find out what it takes to be an astronaut.

Age_____ Sex_____

Education _____

_____

Physical requirements_____

_____

Other requirements_____

_____

Scientific Knowledge Needed _____

_____

What training does a person go through to become an astronaut?

_____

_____

If you are turned down as an astronaut, what other space-related jobs might be exciting? List 6.

1._____ 4._____

2._____ 5._____

3._____ 6._____

(See page 119) SCIENCE FACT AND FICTION / **WS-41**

Name_____ Date_____

CAREERS LIMITED APPLICATION FORM

Imagine that you are applying for one of these careers:

— firefighter	— interior decorator	— used car dealer
— gardener	— astronaut	— dance instructor
— nurse	— secretary	— garbage collector

Select a career and complete the application form.

1. Career choice _____

2. Background experiences qualifying you for the career

_____

3. Knowledge of the career

_____

List types of jobs related to the career.

_____

_____

_____

4. Career performance

Select a job related to the career and describe the steps you would take to do it.   Job_____

First _____

Second _____

Third _____

Fourth _____

Fifth _____

Name_____ Date_____

STITCH-A-SENTENCE

1. Number the words in order for each sentence.
2. Use a needle and thread to sew the words together to make a sentence.

The   bought
girl   a

                                            toy

slipped   silently   the
            seal
                        the   into
harbor.

                    for
                            before   cars
always
                                    street
        watch
                                    you
cross
                        the

the   to
            stitch
time   is   take   Now   a

SPORTS: THE UPS AND THE DOWNS

SPORT:_____

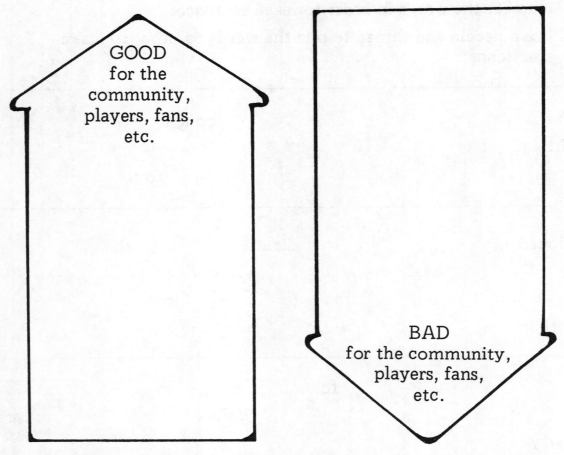

GOOD
for the
community,
players, fans,
etc.

BAD
for the community,
players, fans,
etc.

Write a fact related to each of the topics below. Cut and paste or staple each fact onto one of the arrows shown above. Some facts may seem partly good and partly bad, but make the best placement according to your judgment.

COST TO FANS	EFFECT ON ENVIRONMENT
MONEY PAID TO PLAYERS	RULES
COMMUNITY INVOLVEMENT	HEALTH, FITNESS

Name _____

Date _____

WHAT DO YOU KNOW ABOUT THESE SPORTS?

Sport	Country of Origin	Equipment	Number of Players	Playing Area
Bicycle racing				
Billiards				
Birling				
Croquet				
Curling				
Epee fencing				
Jai alai				
Lacrosse				
Lawn bowling				
Polo				
Quoits				
Rowing				
Rugby				
Shuffleboard				
Skeet				
Squash				

Name _____ Date _____

SPORTS CRAZES AND FADS

1900-1920
BILLIARDS · ICE SKATING · BICYCLING · ROLLER COASTERING · BIRDWATCHING

20s
FLYING · ICE SKATING · BARNSTORMING

Choose one of these sports and design a contest or competition for it.
Fill in the vital facts below.

30s
BULLFIGHTING · MONOPOLY · SKYDIVING · MARATHON DANCES AND

40s
YO-YOING · JITTERBUGGING · SOAPBOX DERBIES · ROLLER SKATING

_____ **CONTEST**

WHAT HAPPENS: _____

_____

_____

50s
ROLLER DERBY · HULA HOOPS · WRESTLING · MOTORCYCLING

RULES: _____

_____

_____

WHERE IT WILL BE HELD: _____

60s
SURFING · SKIING · GYMNASTICS · KARATE · PHONEBOOTH STUFFING · BACKPACKING

_____

QUALIFICATIONS AND LIMITATION FOR
ENTRANTS: _____

70s
SKY DIVING · ROLLER SKATING · TENNIS · RUNNING

_____

_____

PRIZE CATEGORIES   PRIZES

_____   _____

_____   _____

_____   _____

80s
PREDICT SOME SPORTS AND GAME CRAZES FOR THE 80s.

Name _____ Date _____

Name _____

YOU DON'T SAY

You'll need two people for this worksheet. Take a part, YOU SAY or I SAY, and fill in the blanks on your half of the page by writing an antonym for the word underlined in the other person's part. Help each other fill in the blanks. When you have completed the page, read lines to each other emphasizing the underlined words.

I SAY	YOU SAY
1. Let's <u>go</u>.	No, let's _____.
2. I _____ you.	I <u>love</u> you.
3. I like _____ carrots.	I like them <u>raw</u>.
4. I <u>found</u> my roller skate key.	Did you? I just _____ mine.
5. The parking lot is _____.	There's another one that is <u>empty</u>.
6. I think this is a <u>private</u> beach.	No, look at the sign, it says _____.
7. Are we heading _____?	We're traveling <u>south</u>.
8. I <u>forgot</u> to bring home the bacon.	Don't worry. I _____.
9. What a _____ drive.	I think it's very <u>interesting</u>.
10. Don't those flowers look <u>real</u>?	Yes, but I think they're _____.

Select one <u>pair</u> of sentences. Write a continuous dialogue for 2 people using the lines you selected as their first lines. Use as many antonyms as you can in your script.

Name _____ Date _____

For this game you will need:

a friend   a pencil

a die   2 markers (a penny or scrap of paper will do)

To play:

1. Decide which path each of you will take.
2. Roll the die. Move the number of spaces shown on the die.
3. Follow the directions in the square you land on.
4. If your answer(s) is correct, roll the die again to determine your points. Keep a running tally of your score.

The winner is the player with the largest total number of points at the end of the game.

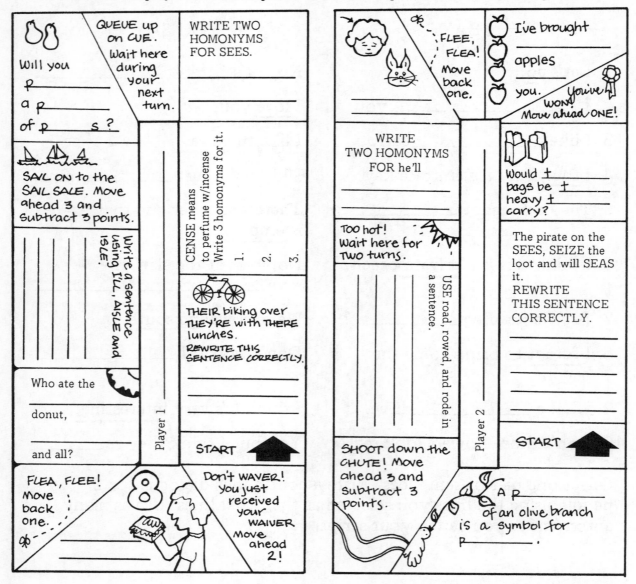

Name _____ Date _____

TRACE-PRACTICE-PERFECT

1. Choose a letter to practice.

2. Have the teacher write it for you.

3. Trace the letter as many times as you need to.

Trace   Practice   Write your
                                                     perfect letter

Name _____ Date _____

Jot·a·story

Jot down your first response to each of these items.

an adjective describing you	a verb describing a funny movement
a noun describing an imaginary object	an adverb describing an awkward movement

a color	a season	a place	a favorite thing

Use all or as many of the responses you have jotted down in one sentence.

_____

_____

Use the sentence you just jotted down as the first sentence in your story. Jot down the rest of your story here.

_____
_____
_____
_____
_____
_____
_____
_____
_____

Index